Creating Discipline in the Early Childhood Classroom

Nancy Leatzow
Carol Neuhauser
Liz Wilmes

Brigham Young University Press

Creating Discipline in the Early Childhood Classroom

REF
LB
1507
.L5
1983

Library of Congress Cataloging in Publication Data

Leatzow, Nancy, 1945–
  Creating discipline in the early childhood classroom.

  Bibliography: p. 171
  1. Education, Primary. 2. Classroom management.
I. Neuhauser, Carol. II. Wilmes, Liz. III. Title.
LB1507.L5 1983   372.11'024   82-17711
ISBN 0-8425-2112-7

Contents

Introduction

According to David Elkind (1980), the major aim of early childhood education is to broaden the child's social understandings. This includes the child's understanding of himself, his peers, adults, and the physical environment.* *Creating Discipline in the Early Childhood Classroom* focuses on the way in which social growth occurring within the early childhood environment leads to the development of discipline.

Discipline is an inner control that balances responsibilities toward oneself and others. It is not a punishment that is done to someone else but is a quality which grows within the individual. The role of the adult is to assist the child in developing inner discipline by creating a supportive environment. This involves an understanding of the social and emotional developmental process as it relates to the child and the adult. It includes the development of adults who have enough self-understanding and self-acceptance to work in a supportive manner with young children as they really are. It requires a classroom environment that provides an appropriate room arrangement, an interesting curriculum, activities that support creative play, and enough trust and security that real problems emerge honestly and are confronted by people who have practiced creative problem solving.

Commitment to this approach allows one to know and enjoy her children. As the nurturing adult works with strength, tenderness, and understanding to guide her children, true discipline emerges.

---

*For editorial purposes, we will use the masculine pronoun to identify the child (unless otherwise specified) and the feminine pronoun for the adult; but we wish to state that references to the child are intended to include both boys and girls and that both men and women assume nurturing roles in the rearing and teaching of children.

One

The Early Childhood Environment

Discipline is an emotionally charged term. Recent Gallup polls indicate that it is the American public's foremost educational concern. Unfortunately, many people equate discipline with punishment, and usage has redefined the term in light of this view. However, the word originates with the Latin word *disciplina*, or instruction. To the early childhood educator, the original definition is consistent with a teaching philosophy based on an understanding of developmental principles. Children are *instructed* in the art of becoming a disciplined person. Their instructors are adults, other children, and the world around them.

Creating Discipline in the Early Childhood Classroom illustrates how proper preparation and execution of the early childhood environment minimizes disruptive behavior and supports positive interactions. When the classroom environment is rich in emotional and social supports, children are able to develop their social understandings of themselves, others, and their world. Children who learn, discover, create, and grow in such an environment are developing self-discipline. This is the ultimate aim of the early childhood educator—to teach children to be internally disciplined individuals. She creates an environment of discipline.

What Is the Early Childhood Environment?

Ruta's child development class is scheduled to discuss "The Early Childhood Environment." On the way to class she thinks about the room arrangement at the day-care center where she volunteers. She pictures the room systematically divided into learning centers. She envisions each learning center and inventories the rich selection of materials. Mentally, she walks through the classroom and notes the child-sized cubbies, the small tables and chairs, open spaces, attractive bulletin boards, and display of children's artwork. When class begins, she feels well prepared to describe an early childhood environment designed to promote optimal learning.

ALYSA STOWE, AGE 8.

As the class discussion evolves, a fellow student presents his concept of an optimal environment. The picture created by Glen is similar to Ruta's, but there is a striking difference. When Ruta thought of the early childhood environment, she limited her vision to a room and its physical properties. Glen's environment is alive. It includes children and adults working together.

Glen listened to the class discussion for some time before adding his point of view. He knows that the physical environment is vitally important and that learning and behavior are influenced by the options built into the room arrangement. However, this is not a discussion of "The Physical Environment"; the subject is "The Early Childhood Environment."

Glen feels strongly that a discussion of environment must include the human factors. He describes not only an extensive block area, but also how Sam and Tracy are trying to balance a complex tower of blocks, while Todd figures out what he can use for turrets on top of his castle. As Glen describes the dramatic play center arranged as a kitchen, his listeners can see Amy and David arguing over who will be the baby. Glen's mental picture includes a teacher seated at the art table collaging a free-form picture and happily talking with a small group of children, while keeping an alert eye on the rest of the room, especially Amy and David. Glen depicts a father putting

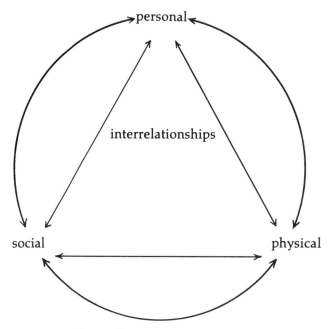

Fig. 1. Environmental Elements

a puzzle together with his daughter, then kissing her good-bye as he leaves for the plant.

The more Glen describes the activity of this dynamic environment, the more Ruta realizes how stagnant her own vision has been. She begins to share Glen's conviction that the early childhood environment includes the richness of people interacting with each other and their world.

As Ruta learned, human environments are made up of three interrelated elements—the personal, the social, and the physical (see fig. 1). Each of these elements is present in the early childhood environment.

The optimal early childhood environment supports the development of self-discipline. It allows a person to feel comfortable with himself, others, and his world. It promotes trust, self-control, purpose, and competence.

The Personal Element

Each child is an environment unto himself. The personal environment consists of a complex collection of emotions, thoughts, and experiences within the individual. Chapter 2 describes Erikson's stages of psychosocial development and illustrates how a child's self-concept is achieved. According to Erikson (1963), children who

4

CHRISTOPHER LEATZOW, AGE 4.

successfully negotiate the major crises of childhood become trust-ful, self-controlled, purposeful, and competent. The early childhood environment supports the development of these positive traits in each child.

The teacher is also an environment unto herself. She is a complex individual whose emotions, thoughts, and experiences directly af-fect her interactions with each child. Just as the child works his way through Erikson's early stages, so the adult works through the stages of human development (see chapter 3, "Development of the Adult"). The early childhood environment supports both the child's and the teacher's development of self-discipline.

An increasing body of research and psychological data demon-strates that children with positive self-concepts are able to solve problems and succeed in later academic settings. The classroom that promotes healthy psychosocial development teaches children to feel good about themselves and to confront problems directly.

To experience empathy and develop meaningful relationships, a person must first understand and appreciate herself. Margaret Mead's autobiography (1972) presents a strong portrait of a child who was wanted and loved by both of her parents. Margaret learned early to trust her mother, who picked her up when she cried, in spite of the child-rearing advice currently in vogue. Her parents and grandmother directed Margaret toward self-control, purpose, and competence. She learned to trust and believe in herself. As an adult, Margaret was comfortable with her role as a woman on the leading edge of contemporary thought. Her early grounding in positive psychosocial development enabled her to conduct seminal research in anthropology, to become a role model to thousands of women, and to devote her life to the study of human nature and the world in which she lived.

The Social Element

Bettye Caldwell (1977, p. 8) has stated, "We need to be as concerned about the development in children of a healthy 'other' concept as we do about the development of a healthy 'self' concept." Neither Dr. Caldwell nor the authors would deny the importance of the development of a healthy self-concept; however, this is only half the goal. Young children also need to construct a healthy other-concept, involving an awareness of and a concern for others.

Any teacher of three-year-old children can describe incidents of parallel play, where two children play at separate games in the same space, each nearly unaware of the other. Yet gradually, as the year progresses, the play takes on a cooperative nature. As children spend more time working together, teachers nurture cooperative attitudes. When teachers express concern for the feelings and rights of each child, children reflect this concern. The seeds of empathetic behavior are sown.

Martie Vincent's classroom demonstrates mutual caring. Martie is a warm human being filled with a sense of wonder about life. She is effective in the classroom because she shares her own love of life with the children. When she fixes a new recipe for dinner, she thinks, "Wouldn't my kids love to make this?" And soon she brings the necessary ingredients and utensils and guides the children through the preparation procedures.

Each child is important to Martie, and each one *feels* important as a result of her interest. She promotes a positive self-concept. She also helps the children to be aware of one another. She emphasizes each child's uniqueness with such statements as:

- "What I like best about these paintings is how different they are, just as you two are each different and special."
- "Did everyone notice that Sally has learned to tie her shoes? All people have something special about them, and today Sally is special because she has figured out how to tie."

DERRICK NEUHAUSER, AGE 6.

- "Rachael can climb to the top of the climber, and Stevie can't. Stevie can put this puzzle together, and Rachael can't. Isn't it interesting how different we all are?"

The children respond to Martie's caring attitude by appreciating one another. Early in the year, when a child approaches the play dough table, Martie walks over and says, "Oh, Tim needs play dough. Everyone break a little off for him." This enables everyone to keep most of what they have. Yet, it provides them with the feeling of taking care of another. In short order, the children follow this procedure without Martie's intervention.

When Jan student taught in Martie's class, she was touched by an expression of empathy between two children. She found them arguing over a fire engine. Each child wanted it very much. Jan said, "You both want it. You cannot both have it. I want you to discuss this problem until you find a solution." The children stopped arguing and, as a result of a short discussion, decided that no matter which one got the fire engine, the other would feel bad. They put the fire engine back on the shelf and found another activity.

Martie's classroom demonstrates the social element in the early childhood environment. As children interact with one another and their teacher, they are developing the foundation of lifelong social attitudes.

ERIC WILMES, AGE 10.

The Physical Element

Kathleen O'Reilly sits over the lunch table explaining the problems involved in teaching the course "Principles of Guidance in Early Childhood Education." Her students are just out of high school. They think kids are great. They are anxious to get into the classroom and solve discipline problems.

In designing the curriculum for the college course, Kathleen has scheduled the first half of the semester to deal with preventive discipline. This includes a consideration of room arrangements that support positive activity and prevent disruption. It includes the planning of curricula rich in age-appropriate activities to stimulate learning and channel energy into acceptable avenues.

Kathleen has seen too many day-care centers "up for grabs" because of poor room arrangement and inadequate curriculum. She has observed active children continuously disrupting young artists at work, simply because the art table was placed too close to the climber. She has helped teachers prevent children from running in open areas by creating "roads" with plastic tape on the floor. She has heard children argue and whine because there are no interesting new activities to challenge and intrigue them.

Kathleen knows only too well from her years in the field that many discipline problems are actually caused by teachers who have not carefully set the stage for their classroom drama. So she is spending a significant amount of time with her college students designing classrooms and curricula, and she grumbles when they cannot appreciate the significance of the exercises. Kathleen wishes that she could magically impart all that she knows to these budding teachers, but all she can do is to lay a foundation for their future. For each of us, learning is a process.

Kathleen's experience illustrates how important it is that the classroom teacher devote time to planning, implementing, and evaluating the room arrangement and curriculum. The relationship between a carefully prepared physical environment and a smoothly run classroom is frequently overlooked. Of course, there is no ideal room design or curriculum that eliminates problems. However, when these elements are calculated to support creative learning experiences, confusion and boredom are minimized and meaningful problems are able to emerge. The teacher is freed to guide her students through the process of creative problem solving (see chapter 10).

Conclusion

The three elements of the early childhood environment—personal, social, and physical—are in a constant state of flux. They overlap and influence one another in their effect on classroom discipline.

Even the seemingly passive child experiences each of these interrelated environmental elements. As Wanda sits in the rocker humming to her doll, she is interacting within her own personal environment. She is affected by the physical and emotional climate of the room. And she is influenced by the social activity around her. She may be unconsciously preparing herself to take a more active role in the social element of the classroom.

The environment of discipline is created by a teacher who prepares the room arrangement and curriculum, supports emotional and social growth, and works in a positive manner to instruct the child in the development of self-discipline.

Two

Development of the Child

The development of discipline within the child is grounded in his view of himself, others, and his surroundings. The process that leads the child to the development of inner discipline is the same process that produces a positive self-image. When nurturing adults have an understanding of the normal psychosocial stages that a child goes through, they are able to create an environment that promotes optimal growth.

This chapter employs Erikson's psychosocial framework to provide an overview of the developmental tasks a child accomplishes in achieving emotional and social maturity. Erik Erikson, an ego psychologist, proposed (1963 and 1968) that emotional and social conflicts occur during normal human development and that each conflict presents an opportunity to make decisions about one's personality. This decision-making process involves the resolution of conflicts that are both emotionally stressful and enriching. Erikson employs the term *crisis* to mean a turning point. Each turning point is both a risk and an opportunity to identify and reconcile the contrasting orientations of the current stage.

Although Erikson has identified eight psychosocial stages that evolve throughout life, this chapter concentrates on the first four stages only, which occur during the early childhood period. Erikson has organized the resolution of tasks according to age periods, has identified a focal crisis, and has projected a specific goal for each crisis. These goals (attributes of personality) form the core of a wholesome personality.

Figure 2 illustrates Erikson's psychosocial stages during early childhood. The initial stage, trust/mistrust, is on the bottom of the chart. The resolution of the first stage is the foundation of the human personality and permeates all other stages. Erikson follows the stage-theorist model, which assumes that each stage is followed in a prescribed order. The child must first resolve conflicts regarding trust/mistrust; then he determines the outcome of autonomy/

Stage	Identifiable Focal Crises	Approximate Age
4	Industry/Inferiority	6–12
3	Initiative/Guilt	3–6
2	Autonomy/Self-Doubt	1–3
1	Trust/Mistrust	0–1

Fig. 2. Erikson's Psychosocial Stages During Early Childhood

self-doubt; thirdly, he sorts out the conflicts of initiative/guilt; and finally he unravels the conflicting issues of industry/inferiority.

Figure 3 graphically demonstrates the results of each psychosocial conflict by placing the extreme choices for each stage on opposite ends of a continuum. As the child works his way through each stage, he travels back and forth along the continuum until a pattern emerges. The goal for each stage is placed above the continuum. The achievement of this goal produces a healthy personality.

The following discussion of Erikson's first four stages explains each focal crisis, states the goal of each crisis, and examines the primary determinants that influence the child's resolution of the crisis. Each progressive stage becomes increasingly complex and is influenced by a growing number of external factors.

Trust/Mistrust (Ages 0–1)

The first psychosocial task the child must resolve is the crisis of trust and mistrust. A person's ability to trust himself and others influences the quality of his experiences throughout life. Trust is the basis of all living and learning. Yet, as crucial as this initial resolution is to one's personality, there are no simple formulas that lead to the development of trust. Nor does one specific incident make a trusting or nontrusting person. An ongoing series of incidents and the child's perception of these experiences determine his view of the world. The primary determinant of trust is adult support.

Adult Support

The child's life begins during prenatal development. His world is the amniotic sac. The child is completely dependent on his mother for sustenance; she nurtures him by caring for herself. She provides a warm, protective, and sustaining environment. The child's view of

COMPETENCE

Stage 4: Industry ------------------------- Inferiority
(feelings of being   (feelings of not
competent)   being competent)

PURPOSE

Stage 3: Initiative ----------------------- Guilt
(feelings of being   (feelings of self-blame
a self-starter)   and of being blamed
                                    by others)

SELF-CONTROL

Stage 2: Autonomy ---------------------- Self-Doubt
(feelings of   (feelings of uncertainty
self-control)   regarding self-control)

TRUST

Stage 1: Trust --------------------------- Mistrust
(feelings of trusting   (feelings of mistrusting
self and others)   self and others)

Fig. 3. Erikson's Stages of Psychosocial Development

the world is determined by the interaction between this environment and his genetic potential. The birth experience provides him with his first sensorial view of a new world and highlights his dependence on significant adults.

Through the early adult/child relationships, the young child learns how to obtain what he needs. The nurturing adult offers immediate gratification. She knows when the infant needs attention and readily provides it. If an adult's attention is slow, the baby cries and the adult relieves the infant's discomfort. Through these early interactions, the child learns to trust significant adults. However, trust develops only when the adult is responsive to the child's needs.

As the infant matures, this secure adult/child relationship enters a new phase. Immediate gratification is no longer provided. The adult allows the infant to wait awhile before fulfilling his needs. This behavior is frustrating and confusing to the child—initially, he has difficulty coping with this change. As time passes, however, he learns that his needs will be met. He understands that the significant adult has other obligations and that he will be cared for. Although the child frequently responds to delays with frustration and anger, the supportive adult eases him through this period and responds to him as soon as possible.

MELINDA NEUHAUSER, AGE 7.

Trust results from the efforts of a consistent, dependable, and nurturing caretaker who prizes and values the child, enjoys doing progressively more difficult activities with him, and is committed to his growth.

Example 1

> While playing at home, John sits on the kitchen floor experimenting with pots and pans. He crawls over to the oven and puts up his hand. His mother says, "Hot, John. Don't touch." John listens as he looks at the oven door. He sees a pot through the glass window. He crawls a little closer. His mother again says, "No, John. Don't touch. The oven is hot." John looks up at his mother and then at the pot in the oven. What will John do? Does he trust his mother, or does he disregard her warning and touch the oven door? Many variables determine his decision.

Placement on Erikson's Trust/Mistrust Continuum

The child's experiences with significant others determine his placement on the trust/mistrust continuum. If the pattern of his

MELINDA NEUHAUSER, AGE 7.

experience is trustworthy, the emerging attitude and outlook is one of confident expectation. His world is perceived as good, stable, and ultimately manageable. His placement on the trust/mistrust continuum is toward the trust end, and his psychosocial personality demonstrates the characteristics of a trustful person.

If the child's pattern of experiences is unresponsive and suspicious, his attitude toward himself and the world is mistrusting and skeptical. He becomes irritable, demanding, and less lovable. This child is positioned toward the mistrust end of the continuum, and his psychosocial personality demonstrates characteristics of a mistrustful person.

Autonomy/Self-Doubt (Ages 1–3)

The second psychosocial task to be resolved is the dichotomy between autonomy ("I'm a separate person") and self-doubt ("Can I live as a separate person?"). The goal of this internal struggle is to provide the child with a sense of control. Building on the established trust, the two-year-old determines how independent he can become and how much control he can have over his environment. He begins to venture out on his own, gradually enlarging his boundaries. These ventures are difficult because of the child's cognitive immaturity and egocentric limitations.

14

The primary determinants of autonomy are adult support and past record.

Adult Support

The primary caretaker "gives the child permission" to develop his autonomy. Without this full support, optimal autonomy is difficult to achieve. Although autonomy is established in many ways, tasks of particular significance are the control of bowels and fears.

Being toilet trained is a visible sign to the young child that he has acquired control over his body. Significant others see the accomplishment of this developmental milestone and generally praise the child.

Adult support allows the child to gain control over some of his fears—separation, abandonment, and darkness. Through the adult's patient guidance, the young child learns to deal more realistically with fearful times. Although these fears continue to cause some internal uneasiness, his emerging sense is continuously gaining control.

Past Record

If the child has positively worked through the trust/mistrust stage, his previous experiences indicate that adults can be trusted and depended on to support his development. He is prepared to develop autonomy and gain control over himself and his environment.

Example 2

> While playing at the park, three-year-old Jesse sees his mother talking with Tom, who is two. Jesse feels angry; "My mom can't play with anyone else." He becomes fearful and thinks, "Maybe she likes him better than me." His mother's response influences Jesse's ability to gain control over his fears. If she understands his jealousy and spends time playing with the two boys, she helps Jesse to see that his initial fear lacked substance. She may be unaware of his feelings, conclude her talk with Tom, and return her attention to Jesse. Repeated experiences of this nature allow Jesse to extend his social world and gain control over his fear. If she punishes his "antisocial" behavior, she may increase his fear and move him toward self-doubt.

Placement on Erikson's Autonomy/Doubt Continuum

Because primary caretakers are not gods or machines, they sometimes respond to a child with warmth and understanding and

MELINDA NEUHAUSER, AGE 7.

sometimes with anger and blame. No singular experience determines a child's placement on the autonomy/doubt continuum. When a child's pattern of experiences allows him to feel in control, he views himself as a person who is able to accomplish tasks on his own. He feels confident and moves toward autonomy on the autonomy/doubt continuum.

When a child repeatedly lacks success or appreciation, he begins to view himself as weak and dependent. He doubts his ability to act on his own and moves toward the self-doubt end of the continuum.

Initiative/Guilt (Ages 3–6)

During the third focal crisis—initiative and guilt—the child is ready to start activities on his own. The goal of this period is a sense of purpose. The child begins to work cooperatively with others and to seek guidance from adults. As he grows physically and cognitively, he develops an increasing sense of his own power. This sense of power allows him to perform many new activities. His play is no longer random. He begins an activity with a goal in mind and has the rudiments of a plan by which to accomplish that goal. The goals and plans may change, but he continues to have a purpose. Play is more than sensorial knowledge and often includes other young children. Thus, the goal of the child is tempered by the plans and goals of others.

The primary determinants of initiative are adult support; past record; opportunities at home, at school, and in the community; and peer influence.

Adult Support

The adult remains an important influence in the life of the child, who continues to seek adult approval. Since the child lacks necessary skills for successful problem solving, he remains dependent on the adult for help in almost every area. The child is beginning to sense his own abilities. However, he is not fully able to take charge.

How primary adults react to the child during his struggles affects the outcome of this stage. If they help him learn to balance his drive for power and play cooperatively with his peer group, adults assist the child to discover initiative. If, on the other hand, they stifle the child's new sense of himself, adults lead him to feel that this new sense is wrong, and feelings of guilt develop.

Past Record

The resolution of the first two psychosocial crises influences this and future stages. Learning to trust adults and feeling in control prepares the child to trust himself and his own abilities. He has developed the necessary inner spirit to take initiative and to begin to trust his ability to deal with everyday situations.

Opportunities at Home, at School, and in the Community

Resolution of the initiative/guilt crisis occurs as most children enter school. The school environment provides unlimited opportunities for the child to exercise his initiative potential. When he perceives himself as functioning independently and achieving successfully, he gains confidence in his own sense of purpose. As these positive experiences are repeated in the neighborhood, at the park, or in whatever situation he finds himself, he learns to trust his own initiative further and to feel good about himself.

Peer Influence

The peer group is just beginning to influence the young child. He is developing an awareness that other children exist and that he must work and play in cooperation with them. The need to balance his egocentricity with his desires for greater sociability is a major challenge of this period. These encounters with peers propel him between initiative and guilt.

MELINDA NEUHAUSER, AGE 7.

Example 3

In an early education center, Tracy is building a sky-scraper. She is in the block corner with Rosa, who is constructing a four-lane highway. Tracy realizes that to complete her skyscraper, she will need additional blocks. She also realizes that Rosa has the necessary blocks. Tracy has many options. Three of them are the following: (1) take the blocks away from Rosa, (2) ask Rosa to join her in the skyscraper project, (3) ask the teacher, who is standing near, to help.

How Tracy solves this dilemma provides clues to her growth in resolving the initiative/guilt crisis. As she works her way through this stage, she alternates between different options until a pattern emerges. Through careful, long-term observation, significant adults may determine this pattern and work effectively with Tracy.

Placement on Erikson's Initiative/Guilt Continuum

As each child works toward resolution of the initiative/guilt crisis, individual patterns develop. The adult observes behavioral clues to ascertain how the child is moving along the continuum. If the child's environment provides opportunities for him to develop a sense of pride in his ability, to seek assistance from supportive adults, to experience successful activities, and to interact with peers, he moves toward the initiative end of the continuum; if not, he develops a sense of overwhelming guilt.

Industry/Inferiority (Ages 6–12)

The fourth psychosocial crisis is the conflict between industry and inferiority. The goal of this internal struggle is a feeling of competence. The child's energies center on achieving competence in the basic tools of literacy—reading, writing, and mathematics. Simultaneously, he learns to control his body through physical activity and develops coordination, flexibility, and strength. As he sharpens these skills through varied and continual opportunities in both domains, he becomes more capable of solving problems and completing tasks.

The primary determinants of industry are adult support; past record; opportunities at home, at school, and in the community; peer influence; failure experiences; and success.

Adult Support

In the preceding stages, the adult's primary role has been to provide emotional support. During resolution of the industry/inferiority crisis, the adult's role begins to change. While the child continues to need emotional support from adults, he now needs adult direction in learning the basic mental and physical skills for problem solving and task completion. As he learns these skills, the child begins to view himself as capable of handling the problems of everyday living. In addition to direct teaching, the adult also supplies the child with freedom to operate independently. She cautiously encourages the child to take risks and to utilize his new skills.

Past Record

As the child develops, his past record becomes increasingly significant. The child who has acquired an optimal sense of trust, autonomy, and initiative is able to concentrate his major energy on the industry/inferiority issue. The child who has tendencies to be mistrustful, doubtful, and guilty continues to work on these issues, as well as on the problem of industry and inferiority. All children have the opportunity to become industrious, but for some it is more difficult than for others.

Opportunities at Home, at School, and in the Community

As the child moves between industry and inferiority, he operates in an increasingly complex environment. Home, school, and the larger community provide a multitude of opportunities for him to practice his new competencies. It is not unusual for a child to feel competent in some areas of his life while feeling inferior in other aspects. It is the pattern that develops over a long term that influences his direction toward industry or inferiority. The child gains a sense of his capabilities as adults allow him to take risks and venture beyond his previously limited boundaries.

Peer Influence

Peers not only play an important role in the child's life, but in some cases their influence is greater than that of the family. Peers are keenly aware of each other's skills, abilities, and physical appearance. During this period, friends tend to be of the same sex, live within a similar geographical area, and have corresponding interests.

Friends see themselves as being alike. They tend to choose a "best friend." Having a best friend and a group of friends provides the child with acceptance and spurs him to solve problems and complete tasks. They challenge him to meet the demands of the group while providing support for his growth. If the child lacks the personal characteristics to belong to a peer group and to have a best friend, he may feel lonely and may develop problems in concentrating on the skills he needs to acquire industry.

Failure Experiences

How the child deals with unsuccessful experiences provides clues to his growth in industry/inferiority. The child takes a strong step toward competence when he is able to perceive his failures as normal steps in the learning process and as opportunities to gain insight and information. Making mistakes is an expected part of problem solving. When significant adults aid the child to see this step as an opportunity for growth, the child accepts it as a natural occurrence and not as a personal failure.

Success Experiences

How the child deals with successful experiences provides clues to his growth in industry/inferiority. When the child's successes are perceived as normal steps of the learning process and as opportunities to gain confidence in his abilities, he gains competence. Significant adults join the child in celebration and express confidence in his ability to continue to build successful experiences based on progressively more difficult tasks.

Example 4

> Tonya, a "bright" child, is falling behind in her school work. She plays on a soccer team and is considered to be the worst player on the team. Her parents feel that her feelings of inferiority toward soccer are affecting the quality of her academic and social experiences. Tonya has a variety of options. She may decide to (1) quit the team and fill her time with more enjoyable activities, (2) remain on the team out of loyalty while putting forth little effort, (3) work as hard as she can to achieve a feeling of competence in the sport.
>
> The ways in which Tonya resolves this and other dilemmas will affect her resolution of the industry/inferiority crisis.

Placement on Erikson's Industry/Inferiority Continuum

The complex factors of the industry/inferiority crisis require a longer period of time for resolution. When a child experiences the acquisition of new skills, greater freedom, friendship that offers challenges and support, and opportunities to view success and failure as normal steps in the learning process, he moves toward industry and develops a sense of competence. When these experiences are lacking or are viewed from a negative perspective, he moves toward inferiority. Children who move from mistrust to doubt toward guilt and finally to inferiority may rework their initial resolutions and achieve the desirable goals of each crisis. However, this possibility becomes increasingly difficult.

Self-Concept

During the resolution of each psychosocial stage, a child's sense of self emerges. Until a child is able to think abstractly (ages fourteen to fifteen), his self-concept defines itself primarily from the quality of the adult-child contact. From the significant adult, and eventually others, he becomes aware of his uniqueness as a person. The resolution of each psychosocial crisis (trust/mistrust, autonomy/self-doubt, initiative/guilt, industry/inferiority) is instrumental in the formation of a child's self-concept. The healthy child emerges as basically trusting, is comfortable with his autonomy and initiative, and perceives himself as an industrious child. This child is also achieving a sense of inner discipline because he feels competent, has purpose, and is in control of himself.

Three

Development of the Adult

The development of discipline within the adult is grounded in her view of herself, others, and her surroundings. Just as the negotiation of the four initial psychosocial crises determines the child's self-concept, so the resolution of the remaining developmental crises produces the self-concept of the adult. An understanding of normal stages of development allows the adult to create an environment for herself which propels optimal growth.

Maria Darrow sits sullenly at an in-service seminar on "Discipline and Child Development." She knows that classroom discipline is related to an understanding of child development, and she feels that she has integrated developmental theory into her classroom environment. She works at enhancing each child's self-concept and instructs him in the complex art of self-discipline.

Maria resents "wasting her time" discussing child development when she would rather be addressing the real problems of teaching. Finally, she interrupts the discussion and attempts to describe her recent struggles.

"I have been teaching for several years, and I think I have a pretty good understanding of child development. But, lately, I haven't been enjoying my teaching as much as I used to. I never feel that I have done enough preparation. I am often irritable and tense. And I notice that when I feel lousy, my expectations for the children change. Their normal noise and activity bothers me. When I'm 'uptight,' I dominate the children and demand greater control. The worst part of all is that when I behave this way, I like myself even less, because I am not allowing the children to be creative and to develop self-discipline."

Maria is startled by her strong statement. She hadn't realized the intensity of her feelings. She is even more surprised by the response of her peers. They understand Maria's frustrations and describe similar experiences.

Stage	Identifiable Focal Crises	Approximate Age
8	Integrity/Despair	56+
7	Generativity/Stagnation	35–55
6	Intimacy/Isolation	19–35
5	Identity/Role Confusion	13–18

Fig. 4. Erikson's Psychosocial Stages During Adulthood

Betty Levy, the consultant in charge of the seminar, can see that these teachers are well grounded in the principles of child development, but she wonders if they have received any training in adult development. As a result of Maria's remarks, Betty suggests that the seminar be expanded to include the full scope of human development. Betty realizes that what Maria and the other teachers need is not more knowledge about children but a greater understanding of themselves as developing persons. She offers to discuss the stages of adult psychosocial development and their relationship to teacher effectiveness. She explains that teachers, as well as children, are in the process of becoming inner-directed, self-disciplined human beings.

Betty employs Erikson's psychosocial framework to provide an overview of the developmental tasks an adult accomplishes in achieving emotional and social maturity. She provides examples to illustrate each crisis.

According to Erikson, the adult proceeds through four major crises, or opportunities to grow and change. He has organized the resolution of tasks according to age periods, has identified a focal crisis, and has projected a specific goal for each crisis. These goals (attributes of personality) form the core of a wholesome personality. Adult attributes of personality build on the previously acquired traits of trust, self-control, purpose, and competence and eventually form an emotionally and socially mature person. Because adult development is a complex issue, only the positive aspects of each stage are examined.

Figure 4 illustrates Erikson's adult stages and the approximate ages of resolution. The fifth stage is at the bottom of the chart and builds on the first four stages identified in chapter 2, "Development of the Child." Stage five, the establishment of identity, is the foundation of the remaining stages, and its influence permeates future development.

WISDOM

Stage 8: Integrity ------------------------Despair

      (feelings of pride   (feelings of disgust
      regarding oneself   regarding oneself
      and one's life)   and one's life)

CARE

Stage 7: Generativity -------------------- Stagnation

      (feelings of being   (feelings of being
      productive)   nonproductive)

LOVE

Stage 6: Intimacy ----------------------- Isolation

      (feelings of affiliation   (feelings of lack of
      with another person)   affiliation with others)

FIDELITY

Stage 5: Identity ------------------------Role Confusion

      (feelings of confidence (feelings of uncertainty
      regarding identity)   regarding identity)

Fig. 5. Erikson's Adult Stages of Psychosocial Development

As individuals mature, deviation from Erikson's model becomes increasingly common. Negative resolution of an earlier crisis slows the process. Adults often need to renegotiate an earlier crisis. It is not unusual for a thirty-five-year-old to be making identity adjustments. Under optimal conditions, the adult resolves her identity (13–18), makes decisions regarding intimacy (19–35), produces generativity (36–55), and attains integrity (56 +).

Figure 5 graphically demonstrates the adult stages with their contrasting choices and resulting attributes. The contrasting choices for each stage are placed at opposite ends of the continuum. Like the child, the adult works through each option by traveling back and forth along the continuum before achieving a sense of internal comfort. The goal for the resolution of each crisis is placed above the continuum. After each goal is achieved, the identifiable attribute becomes an active part of the adult's growing personality.

1   2   3   4   5   6   7   8

Fig. 6. Eight Stages of Psychosocial Development

Figure 6 represents the breadth of human development on one continuum to illustrate the fact that, just as each crisis resolution

24

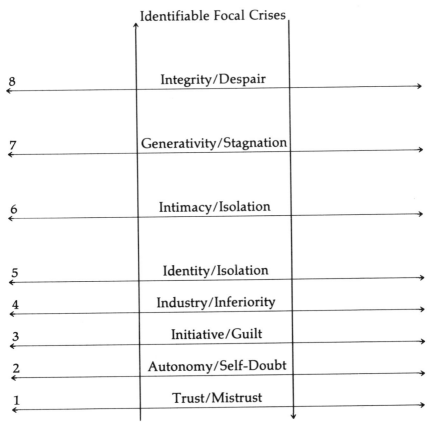

Identifiable Focal Crises

8   Integrity/Despair

7   Generativity/Stagnation

6   Intimacy/Isolation

5   Identity/Isolation

4   Industry/Inferiority

3   Initiative/Guilt

2   Autonomy/Self-Doubt

1   Trust/Mistrust

Fig. 7. Adult Psychosocial Growth Patterns

involves a movement back-and-forth along a continuum, so the scope of development includes back and forth movement. Throughout life, individuals have opportunities to rework a former crisis and to resolve it at a deeper level. Figure 7 pictures this same concept in greater complexity. The horizontal lines indicate backward and forward motion within the age-related crisis. The vertical lines allow for a backward movement, as well as a moving ahead to the next stage.

Backward movement should not be viewed negatively. Life affords many opportunities for the healthy individual to move backward into an earlier stage and resolve it with the assistance of maturing mental faculties and deeper emotional insight.

Of particular interest to the educator is the fact that human relationships evolve according to these same eight stages. The initial crisis of a relationship is trust/mistrust. Once trust has been established, each person experiments to see how much autonomy is allowed. When individuals sense the presence of trust and autonomy, they work at adding initiative and industry to their alliance. When a relationship is characterized by trust, self-control, purpose, and competence, it establishes a unique identity which allows each person to feel intimate and loving. Over years, the relationship becomes generative and caring. It culminates in the achievement and maintenance of integrity.

Whenever an individual embarks on a new interpersonal relationship, she has the opportunity to begin with the initial stage of trust and to work completely through the eight stages of psychosocial development. The person who understands Erikson's stages is aware of the significance of trust throughout life. She works at intelligently trusting herself, others, and the world. She builds a trusting environment to support her growth.

Adult development is internal and involves changes first in perception and then in behavior. These changes occur gradually, often painfully. Just as physical pain informs the person that something is wrong with the body, so mental pain alerts the adult to the need for change. The individual slowly realizes that she has the internal power to make decisions about the quality of her life. While family and friends exert influence, it is the individual herself who must work through the normal crises of life in order to attain a sense of personal identity, intimacy, generativity, and integrity.

Identity/Role Confusion (Ages 13–18)

One of the most difficult tasks in the social-emotional realm is the achievement of a sense of identity. Identity is usually achieved during adolescence, although the identity battle continues throughout life. An identifiable sign of the identity crisis is the person's preoccupation with self. Three major tasks pervade the identity crisis—becoming emotionally independent from parents, achieving a comfortable masculine or feminine social role, and establishing career goals.

An episode on the television show "Happy Days" portrays Joanie, a teenager, taking a step toward independence from her parents. Mr. Cunningham assumes that Joanie will attend the state university where Richie, her brother, went to college. He feels that going to this university is a family tradition and assumes that Joanie will follow in her brother's footsteps. Joanie decides that she doesn't want to go to college. She is not ready to leave home. After as much distress as can be shown in a half-hour television program, Joanie decides to confront her father with her decision. Anger, disappointment, and discussion precede Mr. Cunningham's acceptance of Joanie's decision. Joanie has decided what is best for her, has

DERRICK NEUHAUSER, AGE 15.

confronted her parents with the disparity of views, and has convinced them that she knows what is best. A traumatic emotional encounter for both parents and child has been resolved. This experience moves Joanie a step toward her identity, a difficult task for teenagers with caring parents.

The second task—achieving a comfortable feminine or masculine social role—involves an acceptance of physical changes. Curtis notices that his body is changing. At times, these changes are frightening. The sense of stability that he used to feel through his physical presence has left. He experiences new feelings about his masculinity. His parents tease him about the hair under his arms and his new interest in Jennifer. His dependable favorite, the blue flannel shirt, no longer fits. The sleeves are now up to his elbows, but he rolls them up and wears the shirt. It makes him feel secure.

Determining a career path produces internal anxiety. Much of a person's identification is related to his occupation. Today's complex society and specialization make it difficult to choose a career. Ed would like to be an engineer and plans to attend the state university. Because of the university's selectivity, he must decide as a high school freshman to pursue this career goal. The stringent requirements prohibit Ed from experimenting with alternative career options. This inflexibility may cause internal frustration at a later age,

CARIN PANKROS, AGE 5.

but Ed will work through his conflicting feelings about a career as part of his identity resolution.

Each of these examples illustrates one step in the resolution of identity/role confusion. They are small steps, and the young adult takes many of them (some forward, some backward) before achieving identity. The person who integrates the various aspects of his personality and becomes an identifiable person emerges with characteristics of fidelity, reliability, and authenticity. If the person does not formulate a sense of identity, he experiences role confusion. Eventually, he will have to move backward and establish an identity if he is to achieve personal wholeness. Growth in the next stage—intimacy—will be severely impeded.

Intimacy/Isolation (Ages 19–35)

A sense of identity encourages a young adult to work toward developing an intimate relationship. The primary goal of intimacy is to form a loving sexual relationship with someone of the opposite sex, and the secondary goal is the formulation of nonsexual intimate relationships. Both types of relationships support the adult's emotional growth.

Intimate relationships demonstrate the qualities of trust, autonomy, initiative, industry, and fidelity. Each person communicates his internal feelings and ideals but allows the other space for growth. Each expresses joy when personal growth is demonstrated and shared.

The joy of love begins slowly. Susan notices John in her biology class at the university. He is tall and slender, has light brown hair, and sits in the second row. There is something special about John. His clothes fit perfectly, his posture expresses confidence, and he demonstrates a desire to learn. As he asks the professor a question, his voice is soothing, assertive, and clear. John's enthusiasm for biology rubs off on Susan, and she finds herself spending more and more time studying for this course. She realizes that she also spends more and more time thinking about John. He is becoming important. As the semester progresses, their academic association evolves into a personal relationship.

Both Susan and John have a sense of identity. Their individual identity allows them to work toward developing an intimate relationship and to make a commitment to their relationship. Implicit in the concept of intimacy is equality. The relationship respects and acknowledges each person's area of expertise. It encourages growth without either party feeling inadequate. In John's and Susan's relationship, John's greater achievement in biology does not diminish Susan's feelings about herself. Intimate relationships allow adults to discover varied aspects of another's personality.

Love and trust allow the young adult to feel safe discussing innermost ideas, feelings, and concerns. When personal secrets are shared and accepted by a trusted friend, the young adult is better able to accept herself as she really is.

While Susan and John are studying, Susan says, "John, I am embarrassed to tell you this, but I do not spell very well." John casually replies, "That's okay. Many people can't spell well." Because Susan was self-conscious about her spelling, she had feared that if John discovered this weakness he would like her less. He accepted her perceived disability so casually that Susan became more accepting of it. She noticed that when she wrote a paper she wasn't as tense, and her spelling began to improve.

An intimate heterosexual relationship has these characteristics: trust, autonomy, purpose, communication, acceptance, growth, and love. Personal growth involves dealing with change, and intimacy strengthens the person who experiences and shares these crises.

The second goal of intimacy is to develop intimate relationships without a sexual component. These relationships are built around similar values and support the emotional and social growth of each individual.

CHRISTOPHER LEATZOW, AGE 11.

Carin and Monique have known each other for about five years. They are both professors at a community college and have offices in the same building. Although they are not in the same department, their friendship grew from a shared commitment to academic excellence. They progressed from small talk to discussions of professional concerns and, eventually, to a sharing of personal problems. They manage to snatch moments from busy schedules to share experiences, and these moments are special to both of them.

When Monique's dog died, she borrowed Carin's sunglasses to hide her swollen eyes. When Carin was upset about her teaching schedule, it was Monique who helped her sort through her feelings of anger. When Monique was asked to write a textbook, it was Carin with whom she shared her joy.

Their relationship provides a sense of intimacy. They both trust, care for, and have positive feelings about the other. They communicate their innermost feelings and ideas in an environment of acceptance. This supportive relationship nurtures each person's growth and provides the impetus for generativity.

Generativity/Stagnation (Ages 36–55)

Intimate relationships accommodate a person's need to love and to be loved. When this need is achieved, generativity (caring for others) becomes the major internal thrust. Characteristic of the generativity stage is an internal pressure to produce something lasting or to do something beneficial for others. The scope of human relationships is broadened, and there is movement toward personal wholeness and integrity.

Barbara is celebrating her thirty-fifth birthday. This birthday is full of internal tension. Her mind keeps moving to a recurring theme: "What am I going to do with the rest of my life?" She had planned her life through age thirty-five and had generally followed her plan. She graduated from college, taught school, married, and had children. Now her last child is ready to go off to school. Barbara makes the decision to return to teaching and teaches until she is forty.

At forty Barbara's dissatisfaction is resurfacing. Teaching is not as rewarding as it had been twenty years ago. Her sense of internal pain combined with a feeling of urgency is almost unbearable. She devotes time to making lists, elaborating the advantages and disadvantages of teaching. She attends workshops on career changes, and she reads widely on the subject of career exploration for middle-aged women.

At forty, Barbara has an inward thrust to make decisions and proceed with action. She senses that she must act quickly to achieve a sense of generativity. The internal push is so strong that she struggles to make her life and values congruent. During the resolution of generativity/stagnation, the person finds out who she is and grants herself acceptance. She engages in activities that reflect her values. The generative adult needs deep human contact and no longer accepts a half-lived life. As she completes these developmental goals, she becomes a person with authenticity and integrity.

Integrity/Despair (Ages 56 +)

The person who has achieved integrity communicates inner peace. She is comfortable in diverse situations, and others feel her calm acceptance. Mary Francis Rodale is JoAnn's model of personal integrity. Mary Francis is not beautiful. She dresses oddly. But Mary Francis possesses a sense of integrity. Her presence and spirit exude acceptance of herself and others.

Mary Francis is a professor of early childhood education whose expertise is parent education. Mary Francis is not a parent; she has never married. However, she works successfully with parents from lower-, middle-, and upper-income levels. Parents whose children are blind, abused, and gifted benefit from their interaction with her.

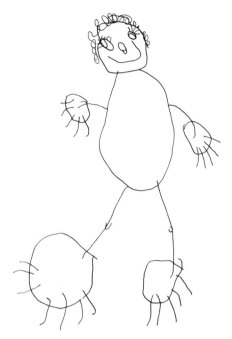

JENNIFER ZAMARIN, AGE 4.

She is able to create an environment between herself and the parent that contains trust and acceptance.

Mary Francis generally starts her professional conversation with the statement, "I'm not a parent. Tell me about it." She listens attentively and nonjudgmentally. The parent grows in self-acceptance and understanding. Mary Francis empathizes with each situation and gives each parent confidence that he or she is capable of dealing with the problem.

When JoAnn sees Mary Francis for the first time in several years, Mary Francis moves next to her, saying, "JoAnn, tell me what you have been doing." JoAnn is embraced in an environment of integrity.

The internal thrust toward integrity becomes more powerful as one ages. The attainment of integrity produces a life full of joy and wonder—a person who is grateful to be alive.

Conclusion

Maria Darrow's attitude at the conclusion of the in-service seminar has undergone a dramatic change from her earlier resentment. She is excited about her initial understandings of adult development and would like to know more. She has gained some insight into herself as a developing person and can see where she stands on the continuum of human growth. She realizes that her own problems can be turned into the impetus for personal growth and that viewing herself as a changing person will make her a more empathetic and effective teacher.

Maria knows that her cognitive development sets her apart from the children and that they count on her to help them express self-discipline. Yet, she shares her children's emotions. Maria decides that both she and the children will benefit from her attempt to be more accepting of herself, to understand and express her honest feelings, and to be willing to open herself to the sometimes painful experience of human growth.

Four

Philosophy of Discipline

Twenty children are seated on the floor around Mrs. Wilson, their teacher, who is holding a flannelboard and conducting a lesson on dressing for cold weather. Bob, the teacher's aide, is preparing a snack across the room. As various children come to the board to "dress" the felt figure, Michael grabs some blocks and bangs them together. The teacher gently tells Michael to put the blocks on the shelf. Michael continues to bang the blocks.

This vignette, or some variation of it, is a common occurrence in the early childhood classroom. Most teachers reading this sketch will respond with a sense of familiarity and will perhaps project themselves into the scene, mentally handling the disturbance. How they handle it will depend upon their beliefs about children and discipline. A teacher in the above described situation has many options. Which option a teacher will choose for responding to Michael's behavior is determined by her philosophy of discipline.

Teachers are called upon every day to respond to the "disruptive" behavior of children. Yet, many teachers are unaware of strategies available for effectively dealing with unacceptable classroom behavior. While specific strategies are examined throughout this book, this chapter focuses on the importance of establishing a philosophy of discipline. It is concerned with the thought process that leads to the determination of deeply held convictions.

When early childhood educators have taken time to ponder their beliefs about children, disruptive behavior is less threatening. The teacher who is in touch with her own philosophical beliefs and feelings about children is able to make quick decisions that are grounded in a carefully considered framework.

A teacher who feels that the primary aim of early childhood education is to help a child feel good about himself will stop disruptive behavior without humiliation, but she *will* stop it—because a child cannot feel good about himself while breaking rules and angering others.

A teacher who believes in the inherent dignity of man supports each child's ability to be competent and looks for ways to turn negative behavior into acceptable activity. A teacher who believes that the major goal of early education is to get kids "hooked on learning" builds on the young child's natural curiosity. When his behavior oversteps the classroom bounds, she helps him to see the importance of working within a logical framework so that learning can continue in a cooperative and enjoyable manner. Ultimately, these philosophical beliefs are determined within the heart of each individual. Yet, there are group experiences available to educators that promote this individual consideration.

The following strategies have been used at early childhood centers to facilitate discussion and individual thought. These strategies assist teachers to examine their beliefs, explore alternative solutions, and understand and empathize with individual children.

Strategy I

Sara Mitchell, the director of a college child-care center, felt that her staff would benefit from a philosophical discussion of discipline. She hoped to encourage each staff member to consider and clarify attitudes toward children and learning. She felt that the staff, which ranged from teachers with advanced degrees to untrained aides, needed a structure on which to base the discussion. Even though the center was noted for its nonstructured, open-ended approach to learning, teachers at the center were traditionally educated and needed a framework to provide a secure starting point. To aid each staff member in determining a philosophy of discipline, Sara designed an instructional strategy that offered individual security and provided for active manipulation of materials. This became the basis for group discussion.

Sara devised a series of eight statements, each expressing a point of view about early childhood education. She selected statements that had a direct or indirect effect on classroom discipline. She then wrote each statement onto a separate three-by-five-inch index card. She needed one set of cards for each staff member. By photocopying each set of cards onto one piece of paper, she minimized her preparation time.

At the next monthly staff meeting, Sara handed each teacher a photocopy of the cards and a pair of scissors. She asked each participant to cut the "cards" apart, read and think about each statement, and then arrange the cards into a pile ranging from the statements most strongly agreed with to statements most strongly disagreed with. Sara specifically avoided using extreme statements, such as "Children need to be spanked" or "All negative behavior should be ignored." Rather, she selected statements within a range of acceptance by the staff. The statements Sara used in this exercise were the following:

- At school, children may choose activities of interest to them.
- Early childhood education offers children opportunities to learn to listen quietly and to take turns.
- Experiencing frustration can be a positive experience.
- Children are more cooperative when rules make sense.
- Children need to know what the teacher expects of them.
- Children are capable of solving their own problems.
- All learning occurs within a structure.
- Teachers are more effective when they communicate with parents.

When each member of the staff had arranged the cards, Sara asked, "Bob, with which statement did you most agree?" As Bob read his statement, Sara wrote it on the blackboard. She then asked if anyone else had selected Bob's statement. Two others had, so she indicated that with two checks after the statement. The discussion evolved naturally from this point. Later, Sara asked Kathy to read the statement with which she most strongly disagreed. Tally and discussion followed. Whenever the conversation lagged, Sara asked, "Which statement did you place as second (third) under strongly agree (disagree)?" Staff members were interested to see the areas of agreement and disagreement.

At the end of the staff meeting, Sara Mitchell was satisfied. Her strategy had allowed each teacher to become involved at a basic, physical level by cutting and arranging cards. Specific ideas were presented for evaluation, which provided some security for each teacher. Since the statements did not represent extreme positions, each staff member needed to examine carefully her own feelings and attitudes before making decisions. Finally, the discussion that ensued was characterized by thoughtfulness, conviction, and creative involvement.

The quality of the discussion can be illustrated by the analysis of the statement, "All learning occurs within a structure." Not surprisingly, most of the staff placed that at or near the "disagree" end of the stack, since they thought of their school as unstructured. However, one staff member, Randy, spoke about what that statement meant to her. She explained that every human encounter has a structure to it. Every day has its structure, and every classroom has its own structure. Randy pointed out that while her classroom appears to be extremely "unstructured," she works hard at structuring an environment where creative learning will flourish. All activities in her classroom are structured by her expectations. She expects the children to play creatively, to solve problems, to respect other children and their work, not to hurt themselves or others. These expectations structure the children's behavior while they are at school. Randy's analysis of the statement caused other staff members to rethink their position.

Because this strategy worked well for Sara and her staff, she extended it at her next meeting. She handed each member of her nine-person staff nine 3-inch by 5-inch index cards and asked each person to write on one card "your deepest conviction about teaching young children." Some of the cards read as follows:

- School is a place where children learn to get along with each other.
- When teachers allow adequate time for planning, children experience optimal learning.
- The most important lesson any child can learn is to like himself!

As each teacher read her statement aloud, others copied it onto one of their cards. Once again, the cards were ranked. The following discussion proved to be stimulating and unifying.

Sara later realized that she had implemented one of her own convictions about learning: "Learning moves from the concrete to the abstract."

Strategy II

Joshua Sampson, a Head Start director, noticed that some of his teaching staff handled disruptive behavior effectively while others appeared frustrated by discipline problems. Joshua felt that there should be some way to share beliefs and strategies among the staff so that the less effective teachers could benefit by the creative solutions employed by others. He spent several weeks observing teachers as they responded to disruptive children. He noted that the most effective teachers:

- Stopped disruptive behavior quickly.
- Responded to individual situations differently.
- Restructured the physical environment to change the child's behavior.

He observed that less effective teachers tended to use a common response to situations, whether or not it was appropriate.

Joshua decided to conduct a series of staff meetings where specific discipline problems would be described and possible solutions presented. His goal was to enable teachers to see that for every problem there are many possible solutions. He felt that thinking about options ahead of time would enable teachers to respond appropriately and to feel better about themselves professionally.

At the first staff meeting, Mrs. Wilson described the situation related at the beginning of this chapter—Michael's disrupting group time by banging blocks together. The staff was encouraged to brainstorm as many solutions as they could. The following options were suggested:

1. Mrs. Wilson moves next to Michael and sits down. She takes the blocks, sets them on the shelf, and lightly rests a hand around Michael's shoulders as she continues her activity with the group.

2. Mrs. Wilson asks Michael to come up and "dress" the flannelboard figure and then sit down next to her.

3. Mrs. Wilson asks Michael to come up and hold the flannelboard for her.

4. Mrs. Wilson says, "I can see that Bob needs help fixing our snack. Carol and Michael, please walk over to Bob and see what he would like you to do."

5. Mrs. Wilson says, "The blocks need to stay on the shelf for now. Bob, could you please push the block shelf out of Michael's way?"

6. Mrs. Wilson and Bob confer later. If Michael is repeatedly disrupting group time, they may decide that he is not developmentally ready for this activity. In the future, Bob provides an alternative activity for Michael during group time.

7. Mrs. Wilson and Bob change the room arrangement, eliminating blocks, toys, and other distractions from the group-time area.

8. Mrs. Wilson says, "Oh, Michael, you've found the talking blocks. Bring them to me and sit here until this game is over. When everyone has had a turn at the flannel board, you can show the class how to make the blocks talk, and we will play a rhythm game."

9. Mrs. Wilson says in a singsong voice, "Mike, Mike, Mike, put the blocks, blocks, blocks on the shelf, shelf, shelf and come here, here, here. I have a secret to tell you!" She whispers to Mike that after snack she will let him teach the class how to make music with the blocks. She then laughs and tells the class, "Mike and I have a surprise for you later on!"

10. On future days, Bob makes certain that Michael has participated in some physical activity, such as climbing or jumping games or a run around the playground just before group time, so that he has had a chance to "get the wiggles out" before sitting still.

The staff was pleased with their ability to think of so many solutions that were supportive of Michael. Each suggestion could quickly stop Michael's disruptive behavior without humiliating him in

38

MELINDA NEUHAUSER, AGE 4.

front of his peers. The staff agreed that Michael had probably discovered an activity more interesting to him than the teacher's. However, since his activity interrupted others, it needed to be stopped.

Joshua Sampson realized that teachers do not change quickly and that meaningful change requires continuous support. He continued to schedule staff meetings that anticipated and provided solutions for classroom difficulties. The staff appreciated the brainstorming sessions and began to respond to children in more inventive and appropriate ways. These sessions also opened communication among the staff. Teachers spent increased time discussing discipline strategies and teaching procedures on an individual basis.

Strategy III

Each fall Ruth Brown gives her teachers two months to become acquainted with each of the children in their classes. At the end of October, she holds a teachers' meeting and requires each teacher to be prepared with the following goals: (1) one educational goal for the academic year—what the teacher plans to accomplish with the whole class, and (2) one long-range goal for each child in the class— what the teacher plans to accomplish with each child during the year.

The educational goals are discussed at the meeting. Ruth believes that, as each teacher decides on one educational goal for the year, she is forced to consider her own beliefs and to decide: "What do I most want to do for these children?" "What do I expect my students to gain from this year?" When a teacher has made that decision, it gives each activity and each school day a focus. It gives the teacher a sense of purpose. The discussion of these goals provides an opportunity for the staff to consider the school's purpose and to reach a philosophical agreement of that purpose.

At the end of the meeting, Ruth schedules a conference with each teacher to discuss individual student goals. As the teacher formulates a specific goal, she gains insight into the child's nature and is able to work more effectively with him.

At Ruth's conference with Nancy, each child in the class is discussed. Nancy explains why she established each goal. Ruth adds information about families, as she has enrolled older siblings in the school. Examples of Nancy's individual student goals are the following:

- Peter—to help Peter feel comfortable at school and to work through his separation anxiety.
- Carla—to help Carla relax and eventually be able to sit through a group time.
- Tommy—to support his positive self-concept and to provide him with a rich learning environment.
- Shelly—to find ways for this quiet child to relate to the other children.
- Matthew—to help Matt develop some control over his behavior and find acceptable ways of expressing himself.

Completing this exercise enabled Nancy to be more effective in the classroom. For instance, another teacher might have reprimanded Matthew when he yelled at Carry, "You dummy! Give that back to me." But Nancy moved next to Matt, shook his hand, and said, "Matt, it makes me feel so good that you are talking to Carry instead of hitting him. You are really learning to control yourself." Because she had a clearly defined goal for Matt, she was able to recognize his behavior as a step toward the development of internal control. Matthew became aware of his progress because Nancy labeled it for him.

Peter's behavior at school could be described as passive. He remained apart from other children, sitting in the small rocker or doing a solitary art project. One day, he burst into tears, quietly sobbing, "I want my mommy." Remembering the goal she had established for Peter, Nancy welcomed this outburst as evidence of growth. Peter was moving from passivity to an ability to understand

and express his feelings. Nancy asked Ruth to cover the class while she spent twenty minutes with Peter on the porch swing. She said, "I know it makes you sad to leave your mom. You are sad, and you need to cry. I'll sit here with you while you cry, and when you are done, we will go inside." Because Nancy realized that this was the major learning experience of Peter's year, she gave him the time and attention he needed.

Strategy IV

The final strategy for determining a philosophy of discipline is aimed at increasing empathy. This teaching strategy requires teachers to spend time in the center interacting with the environment in a playful manner to gain some understanding of how the children feel when they are at school.

Each school year, Karen Swanson schedules a time for her teaching staff to meet at school and spend an hour playing in a classroom. Members of the teaching staff involve themselves in creating art projects; building with blocks; woodworking; and playing with table games, building materials, sand, and water. Some even engage in dramatic play, sitting in the kitchen over a "pretend" cup of coffee. Each year Karen assigns a few roles to add a touch of "reality." For instance, as Mark and Beth build a complex ship with large blocks, Irene casually walks past and knocks it down. Just when Jess is enjoying the play dough, Yvonne grabs it from him. Finally, at a point when everyone is engrossed, Karen announces, "It's time to clean up." She insists that everyone stop immediately and clean up.

After this experiential exercise, coffee is served and everyone sits down to share their feelings and responses. Every year there is a discussion of the therapeutic value of the experience. Someone usually suggests that they open the center at night and offer classes for harried adults who could unwind over blocks and collage. The staff generally feels that this activity helps them to better understand the children with whom they share their days. Teachers who have experienced the frustration of a toppled construction or of having to clean up an engaging project on command are more understanding and patient with children in similar situations.

Conclusion

These four strategies illustrate how teachers work together to determine a philosophy of discipline. While group brainstorming sessions have a synergistic effect, individual brainstorming sessions are also necessary. Everyone needs time to think. A teacher who cares about herself makes time for contemplation.

Effective teaching is grounded in philosophical conviction. A teacher is required to make important, spontaneous decisions throughout the teaching day. She stops disruptive behavior, suggests alternatives, and employs logical consequences. She is able to handle these situations with confidence because she has established a philosophy of discipline.

Five

The Physical Environment

Students of human behavior don't exhaust themselves trying to determine whether man is inherently good or evil; they concentrate on the conditions that make it possible for the good to emerge. . . . The job of truly reasonable persons is to create and enlarge those conditions which make progress possible, and to arrest or change those conditions which make disintegration inevitable. [Cousins 1981, pp. 69, 70]

While an individual's environment includes both physical and human conditions, this chapter focuses on the physical conditions that promote the development of self-discipline in the early childhood environment. It emphasizes "conditions that make it possible for the good to emerge" and looks briefly at "those conditions which make disintegration inevitable." A rich, nurturing environment, arranged into learning centers, frees children to explore, invent, and construct knowledge; it enables teachers to provide, support, and extend learning.

Yet, the importance of the physical environment is often overlooked. It is possible for individuals untrained in early childhood education to look at classrooms without understanding the effect of the physical conditions that inevitably lead to either progress or disintegration. According to Phyfe-Perkins (1981, p. 31), "By being aware of the effect of the setting on behavior, teachers can intervene to prevent problems, reduce the density of children, or otherwise arrange the environment to support the behaviors desired." Planning the physical environment is an important aspect of preventive discipline.

Mava Reynolds is student teaching at her community college laboratory school. She also works as an aide at Happy Time Day-Care Center. Since Mava started her internship at the college, she has been bothered by the behavior of the children at Happy Time. One afternoon at student teaching seminar she expresses this concern: "I don't understand how the children at Happy Time can be *so different* from the children at the lab school."

Dr. Thompson, the college instructor, asks Mava to describe how the children differed.

"Well, you know how they are here, so involved. They aren't quiet exactly, but they are calm, hardly ever yelling or running. They have fun but seem to be more serious about their work or play. It seems like the kids at Happy Time are always running around and yelling. They throw toys and fight. They whine. Their play seems sort of frantic, and they jump from one activity to another."

"How do the teachers deal with the behavior you have described?"

"Most of the time they ignore it. I think it's just so frustrating for them. I figure that the kids act that way because of their families and that the teachers just feel helpless. But when I think about it, the parents there don't seem any different from the parents here at the lab school."

"Maybe there are some differences in the two facilities that influence the children's behavior. Are the classrooms arranged differently? Why don't you try to describe them?"

As Mava describes the classrooms, it becomes evident that there are major differences between them. The laboratory school is divided into learning centers. The equipment is logically arranged on low shelves. Careful thought has been given to the flow of traffic. Child art is attractively displayed on the walls. While the overall structure of the room remains constant, the classroom seems to grow and change with the teaching units and the children themselves.

While the classroom at Happy Time also has equipment available on low shelves, the materials are not logically organized, nor are spaces divided into separate centers. Blocks, which require a large, active play space, are on the same shelf with puzzles, which suggest quiet work at a table. Long, open spaces in the room invite the children to run. The walls are stark, except for one bulletin board with commercial pictures of children expressing different feelings. The room appears the same as it had months ago, without the addition of new equipment.

This discussion illustrates that the overall room arrangement in the early childhood classroom exerts a strong influence on the behaviors of both children and teachers. An effective room arrangement prevents disruption and supports self-discipline. It allows "the good to emerge."

Just what is this ideal physical arrangement that offers such positive results? It would be convenient if there were a simple formula for that utopian environment where everyone is happy, confident, and cooperative. But, of course, each teacher needs to develop her own "conditions" that feel comfortable, conform to the available space, and meet the needs of the children. Dr. Thompson comments that it took the laboratory school staff two years to arrange an optimal learning environment.

To develop self-discipline, young children must be able to interact with their environment—to move, talk, manipulate, rearrange, create, and play. In order to provide an environment that allows children to explore with their bodies, their minds, and their senses, most early childhood facilities are arranged around the learning-center concept. Learning centers are structured areas within the classroom designated for specific types of learning and play.

The effective teacher allows time to think and to plan for the best room arrangement. Some teachers take pencil and paper to diagram a room arrangement before moving furniture. Others need to spend long periods of time in the room, feeling and experiencing it, before a solution is evident. Others simply move furniture and equipment.

This chapter describes eight primary learning centers and four auxiliary centers. When the classroom is large enough, all eight primary centers are provided. However, when space is limited, a teacher may need to select the centers that seem most appropriate to her situation and realize that centers can be rotated.

In planning the location of learning centers, teachers consider the location of lighting sources, storage cabinets, bathrooms, water sources, exits, wall space, bulletin boards, and doors to the outside play area. When a teacher knows the children who will be interacting with the environment or has access to information about them, she provides for the needs and interests of specific children.

Learning centers are placed so that the logical traffic flow moves around, not through, them. Long expanses of space are broken up by the placement of learning centers and furniture. When this is not possible, colored plastic tape can be used to create paths that wind around and through the spaces. Children are directed to move between the tape. These paths provide a natural slowing and purposefulness to the children's movement.

Once the centers are established, the overall effect is considered. The room should feel comfortable. It may need additional softening through the addition of such items as a child-sized rocker, an overstuffed chair or a couch, cushions, or stuffed toys. It may need to be more aesthetically pleasing through the addition of appealing colors, posters, or displays. Some wall space, however, should be left

AMY GILL, AGE 5.

open for displaying the children's artwork. Additional room enhancements relate to the current teaching unit.

Primary Learning Centers

These eight learning centers prevent disruptive behavior and support the development of self-discipline. They provide a balance of activities and equipment with which the young child may interact. Learning centers allow for individual as well as group experiences. They divide the overall classroom space into quiet and active areas. Learning centers offer children a choice between the creative opportunities of open-ended activities and the security of self-correcting equipment. They invite children to become involved.

Creative Art Center

In the art center, supplies are usually grouped on a shelf or a special cart next to the art table. Smocks are hung where children can reach them. Convenient drying space is provided for artwork. Supplies are introduced gradually and are rotated throughout the year. Some children choose to shape, mold, and poke play dough or clay. Others collage art scraps, noodles, or small sensory materials. Still others may decide to paint with tempera, water colors, or finger paints. Blank paper, crayons, magic markers, and pencils are also available. These art activities help children to develop fine motor control and eye-hand coordination, practice conservation of materials, and engage in symbolic representation. Frequent interaction with the art center allows children to express emotions, to discover alternative solutions to problems, and to unlock the creative potential within themselves. The art center promotes disciplined creative involvement (see chapter 9, "Creativity").

Dramatic Play Center

The dramatic play center is usually planned around a home-related theme, which allows the child to explore and practice interpersonal skills through role playing. Throughout the year, equipment in the center is changed to coordinate with the current teaching unit; for example, if the teaching unit is weather, the dramatic play center may become a beach by adding a plastic swimming pool, sunglasses, and towels. Through dramatic play activities, children are able to organize, synthesize, and express their observations of the world. They practice symbolic representation. They are able to experience an assortment of roles, including those of authority figures, and to practice reciprocal communication. Creative dramatic play leads to the resolution of interpersonal problems under the teacher's guidance.

Manipulative Center

The manipulative center is characterized by equipment that helps young children strengthen their small muscles, use their creative abilities, and expand their communication skills. Examples of equipment located in this center are puzzles, small blocks, board games, lacing boards, stacking and nesting blocks, peg boards, and dressing frames. When manipulating concrete objects and participating in board games, children work individually or in small groups. The manipulative center introduces the concept of games with rules. As children interact with manipulative equipment, they strengthen their memory, their small muscle coordination, their awareness of positive and negative space, their knowledge of whole-part relationships, and their problem-solving abilities. They develop a sense of autonomy and competence.

Large Muscle Center

The area designated for the active or large muscle center depends on available space. In some facilities, classrooms share a common space, rotating its use. Other facilities have a large muscle center in each classroom, and still others schedule most of their large muscle activities outside. Climbers, balance beams, individual trampolines,

GREGORY WILMES, AGE 7.

mats, balls, and riding toys are typical pieces of equipment in a large muscle center. Skills acquired in this center help young children strengthen their physical coordination, balance, locomotive abilities, and awareness of themselves in space. The large muscle center prevents discipline problems by providing a constructive outlet for the abundant energy of young children.

Block Center

The block center is a special place where children can construct and "destruct" their own work. Unit blocks are the most common type of blocks located in this area. In addition, the block center might have cardboard blocks, hollow blocks, planks, block people and animals, trucks, cars, fire engines, and other accessories to help the child's imagination come alive. Through block play, children become attuned to balance, patterns, size, dimension, spatial relationships, and architectural construction. Children begin to assimilate the concepts of seriation and reversibility. Just as they learn to control the blocks and accessories, children begin to control their own impulses.

Language Center

While the entire early childhood environment facilitates the development of communication skills, it is appropriate to set up a

ERIC WILMES, AGE 10.

specific learning center with books and equipment that promote language. Flannel-board pieces and a large flannel board, puppets, giant posters and films, and a record player with records can all be a part of a well-developed language center. A variety of books that are continually rotated is another key ingredient. A specific place is also designated for child-constructed books. The children are allowed to view, hear, manipulate, and assimilate the properties of their native language. Through activities in the language center, children acquire the foundations for reading readiness, which include listening and speaking skills, vocabulary development, and concept formation. Language mastery is a major developmental step toward self-discipline, as it allows children to resolve their problems verbally.

Science Center

The science or discovery center provides children with opportunities to examine a variety of interesting objects, plants, and classroom pets. Simple scientific equipment is available, such as magnifying and minifying glasses, balance scales, sorting trays, magnets, and simple machines. Children enjoy bringing special objects from home. In the science center, children heighten their sense of awareness, develop their observation skills, learn to classify and organize data, and gain the ability to communicate knowledge. This scientific awareness leads to observation, competence, and cooperation.

Outdoor Center

A teacher who views the playground area as an outdoor learning center is more attuned to potential learning opportunities. This center is expanded and coordinated with ongoing teaching units just as is the language or art center. When weather permits, the day's focus can shift to the outdoor center. This area becomes the classroom, complete with its own individual learning centers. Art materials can be moved to outside tables, where spilled paint simply colors the grass. An outside science table allows children to examine objects from the natural world in the natural world. Books can be leafed through under a leafy tree. As children explore the potentials of sand, climbing apparatus, riding toys, balls, and mazes, they are able to exercise with little restraint. They strengthen and coordinate their whole bodies. They interact with the outdoor world, and they expand their imaginations and curiosity. Their enjoyment of the outdoors leads to a healthy self- and other-concept.

Auxiliary Learning Centers

A well-developed program for young children incorporates opportunities to explore the properties of sand and water, to be involved in simple cooking experiences, to build and construct, to sing, dance, and move to music. While these learning experiences play a vital role in the program, they do not need to occupy a permanent space in the classroom.

Sand/Water Center

Some early childhood facilities own a commercial sand and water table, which becomes a permanent learning center. However, there are other ways to introduce sand and water into the environment. Some facilities provide tubs or dishpans filled with sand, water, or related materials, such as rice, sawdust, dirt, or gravel. These tubs are set on the art table or added to the manipulative center. Other facilities offer a small plastic swimming pool filled with sand or water, which is placed on the floor in the block center. As children manipulate these materials, they internalize conservation behavior. These experiences are open-ended and relaxing and aid children not only to expand their sensory awareness but also to feel comfortable with themselves and others.

Cooking Center

Cooking activities may occur in a cooking center or in an area allotted to cooking for a specific period of time. Cooking enables

CHRISTOPHER LEATZOW, AGE 11.

children to integrate and apply a variety of learning skills, as they "read" the recipe, measure ingredients, stir, spread, pour, and observe basic physical changes. Cooking in small groups requires children to wait their turn and to cooperate. They understand the necessity of collaboration.

Construction Center

A construction center may focus around a workbench, where children learn safe and proper use of hammers, nails, measuring tapes, and other tools. However, construction-type activities are as varied as scrap wood sculpture in the art center, rock constructions at the science table, or cardboard box groupings in the block center. As children build and rebuild with a variety of materials, they develop whole-part, sequential, and spatial relationships. Their active involvement allows them to experience rewards from the work itself and to develop purpose and competence.

Music Center

A music center may be available for self-directed activities such as listening to records and tapes or playing rhythm instruments. Music and movement, however, tend to flow spontaneously from many children and are integrated into the program, as children

JENNIFER GILL, AGE 9.

chant, rhyme, dance, and experiment with pitch and tone. These musical explorations aid in the development of listening and language skills necessary for later reading. They enrich children's poetic and aesthetic sensibilities. Children act out their impulses in a positive manner.

Evaluation

Once a classroom is arranged and learning centers established, the teacher observes the children at work. Having invested time and thought to the physical room arrangement, the teacher gives it time to work. However, emerging patterns may necessitate some changes. If a particular center is frequently crowded, it needs to be expanded or adjusted to limit the number of children allowed inside. Unused centers can become more appealing by the simple introduction of a new piece of equipment to stimulate interest.

Conclusion

A major aspect of preventive discipline is the preparation of the physical environment. The classroom arrangement exerts a strong influence on behavior. When teachers take the time to arrange a logical, varied, and stimulating environment, they minimize behavior-related problems.

Early childhood classrooms arranged in learning centers promote autonomy in the child. They encourage self-selection of task, high-level involvement, and internally controlled behavior. Ultimately, a supportive environment invites children to acquire knowledge and practice creative problem solving. It communicates trust, respect, and confidence in the child. It nurtures positive behavior and self-discipline.

Six

Curriculum

Preventive discipline includes preparation of the physical environment and the curriculum. When these two elements are designed in accordance with principles of human development, learning centers that enrich and delight and activities that stimulate and challenge enable children and adults to interact in a positive manner. Self-discipline is supported.

The early childhood curriculum is neither idle play nor a pushing down of elementary school academics. It requires an understanding of how the young child thinks and learns. A meaningful curriculum supports the child's desire to understand the world around him and his place in it. It instructs through a variety of experiential activities that extend and enrich the child's natural tendency to play, organize, invent, and construct. The curriculum promotes the growth of social understandings.

As a college student, Liz Smith decided that when she became a teacher she would be flexible and creative and would allow her students options and choices. She would not be a highly structured teacher or have a teacher-directed classroom. She was determined to provide her students with the type of learning environment that she would have appreciated in school.

Finally, Liz had a classroom of her own. No longer did she have to conform to the standards of her college professor, whom she felt to be too structured. Her teaching would be her art.

Liz decided to plan her first unit around shells. On a recent trip to Florida she had collected and brought home a large variety of shells. She knew that kindergartners are generally interested in shells. She was certainly interested in them—they brought back happy memories.

Liz kept her curriculum planning simple. It consisted of three objectives: (1) discussing and showing the shells; (2) putting shells in the art center to create with, to paint, and to glue; and (3) putting shells in the science center and sand/water center to discover and manipulate. She intended to keep teacher direction to a minimum.

Her goal was to allow the children to decide what they would like to do.

As the independent exploration time progressed, Liz knew that something was wrong. Susan was throwing shells at Bill and Sandy. Melinda was riding the tricycle over the shells to make concrete for a road. Nawanna was painting shells in the cubbies and was dripping paint over the children's coats and hats.

While Liz viewed herself as child-centered and a provider of creative opportunities, instead she demonstrated an ignorance of the principles of curriculum and a disrespect for her children. Teachers demonstrate respect for the young child's ability to express creativity and self-discipline by carefully preparing the physical elements of the environment. The environment of discipline is only truly disciplined when it offers a rich assortment of age-appropriate activities. An examination of the curriculum planning conducted by another first-year teacher illustrates these fundamental principles.

Mary Alice woke up energized. It was the first day of school, and she was anxious to meet her students. She dressed quickly and arrived at her classroom an hour before school started. She walked through the classroom door. Her heart was pumping at an alarming rate. She glanced around the room; everything was as she had left it. The physical environment was well planned and intellectually stimulating. She had brought fresh flowers and placed them in a vase on the table in the housekeeping corner. The flowers signified the final step in her educational planning or curriculum.

Mary Alice has spent innumerable hours preparing for optimal student learning. Her planning is part of what educators define as curriculum. Curriculum is a broad-based system that aids the teacher to determine (1) what students learn, (2) what experiences should be provided, (3) how these experiences are organized, and (4) how to evaluate student learning. Curriculum is a road map that provides definite guidelines for both the teacher and the student.

What the Student Should Learn

Mary Alice knows that time invested in curriculum planning will pay its dividends in the classroom. She began her planning by determining *what the students should learn* during the academic year. In order to make this determination, she gathered appropriate data and wrote out her educational goals. The background information necessary to the formulation of educational goals can be classified according to the following categories:

- Developmental abilities of the learner. (What is he capable of learning?)
- Societal expectations. (What do parents, the school, and society expect the student to learn?)

- Content/subject matter. (What segment of knowledge will be studied?)

To gather the necessary data, Mary Alice read developmental charts, individual student records, and information about her school. She spoke with fellow teachers and visited community sites. She read curricular materials and inventoried equipment.

Figure 8, "Determination of Educational Goals," details the steps that Mary Alice took in gathering her data. It describes both the

Activity	Purpose
Developmental Abilities of the Learner	
Read developmental charts of 4-, 5-, and 6-year-olds to provide general guidelines for physical, emotional, social, and cognitive growth.	Determine general parameters of child's growth and development.
Read individual student records.	Become acquainted with individual students, their strengths, and identifiable handicaps.
Societal Expectations	
Read information about school and tour physical plant.	Ascertain goals and available services within school.
Talk with fellow teachers about school philosophy, community presumptions, and parental backgrounds.	Develop awareness of school, community, and parental expectations.
Visit Chamber of Commerce and library. Read newspaper and telephone book for information about community services.	Determine available community facilities that support educational program.
Content/Subject Matter	
Read available curriculum guides, learning units, and lesson plan books.	Review previous educational experiences and suggestions of other teachers and construct alternative learning experiences.
Inventory classroom equipment and additional learning materials available in school.	Become aware of available educational equipment.

Fig. 8. Determination of Educational Goals

58

activity and the reason for the activity. It classifies each step according to the preceding categories.

After reviewing her information or data, Mary Alice determined what her goals would be. Educational goals are general and provide broad direction. Mary Alice's goals for her kindergarten class are the following:

- To promote a positive self-concept.
- To enhance language arts skills.
- To gain and improve self-maintenance skills.
- To provide concrete experiences in math/science.
- To promote social-interaction skills.
- To participate in art and music experiences.
- To improve large and small muscle coordination.

Once the goals were determined, Mary Alice decided upon thematic units of study, such as animals, family, and holidays. She determined, by consulting the school calendar, the time placement of each unit. (Some units are one week in length, while others are two or three weeks. The organization of these units for the entire academic year is called the year-long curriculum. Even when the year-long curriculum is predetermined, the teacher needs to establish educational goals and to understand how each unit relates to these goals.)

What Experiences Should Be Provided

When a teacher has determined what the students are to learn, she moves to the second step of curriculum planning—*what experiences should be provided.*

Before presenting a unit to the class, the teacher gathers materials and resources. She begins to write down activities to include in the unit. During the summer Mary Alice began to organize a unit on sand, stones, and shells. She accumulated ideas and then organized them according to learning centers and group experiences. Mary Alice prepared the following unit, "Sand/Stones/Shells."

Learning Centers

Language Center
- Make a tape of the book, *Everybody Needs a Rock*, by Byrd Baylor. Set the book, tape, and recorder in the language center.
- Check out a filmstrip from the library about sand, stones, and shells.
- Show slides from vacation in California.
- Display reference and story books in the Language Center.

Science Center
- Put stones, shells, and sand on the science table. Use three plastic tubs or aluminum pans. Let the children examine them with a magnifying glass.
- Put out only the stones or the shells. Have two empty containers on the table. Encourage children to sort the stones or shells into two piles. The only rule is that each pile has to have something about it that is the same.

Manipulative Center
- Partially fill three one-pound coffee cans—one with sand, one with stones, one with shells. Encourage the children to shake them and guess what is inside.
- Set out the box of stones for the game "Get to Know Your Stone."
- Stone Sorting: Glue five or six shells onto a piece of posterboard. Have a pail of stones near the game board. Encourage the children to create categories for the stones and place them in the shells.
- Stone Counting: Have small stones available. Make a counting board by writing the numeral 1 on a piece of posterboard. Draw a dot under the numeral. Then write the numeral 2 with two dots beneath. Repeat to ten or twenty. The children put one stone on each dot and count as they go.

Dramatic Play Center
- Convert the dramatic play area into a beach. Add the following items:
  - A wading pool
  - Beach towels
  - The sand/water table
  - Pails, shovels
  - Rubber rafts and other water toys
  - Bathing suits
  - Small picnic table and bench (if possible)

Block Center
- Put butcher paper onto the area floor. Let the children paint the water and sand area of the beach. They can build on the "beach" and in the "water."

Outside
- Add a tub of miniature toys to the sand area. Include cars, trucks, boats, people, animals.
- Make water available. Wet sand stimulates a new type of sand play.

GREGORY WILMES, AGE 7.

- Supply combs of varying sizes and shapes. Encourage children to make patterns.
- Get a sturdy stool. Let the children jump into the sand.
- Bring the water table outside. Let the children scrub stones and shells.
- Get three large plastic containers, all the same size. Fill one with coarse sand, one with fine sand, and one with pea gravel. Pour water to the top of each container. Put the containers in the sun. Watch the containers and see how long it takes the water to disappear in each one. Which one absorbed the water first? Last?

Art Center
- Make stone sculptures. Collect lots of stones. They can be different sizes (flat ones work the best). Using white glue and meat trays, let the children build designs with the stones. Let the designs dry overnight. *On the next day,* dilute more white glue with water and let the children "paint" the glue all over the meat tray and the stone sculpture. This adds a shiny finish to the design.
- Enjoy glue designs. Use colored construction paper and squeeze-bottle glue and let the children squeeze a glue design all over the paper. Next, have them sprinkle sand over the glue. Salt shakers with large holes work well. Shake the excess sand into a pan.

- Enjoy glue designs another way. Make colored glue by adding dry tempera paint to the white glue and stirring thoroughly. Brush the colored glue onto white paper. Once again sprinkle the sand onto the glue design. Shake off the excess sand.
- Using colored glue, make a collage with shells on heavy cardboard.
- As a final art project, let the children have a combination of sand, stones, and shells. Let them collage the materials onto a large meat tray or cardboard.

Group-Time Activities

Finger plays
Ocean Shell

I found a great big shell one day,	(Hold hands cupped as if holding a large shell.)
Upon the ocean floor.	
I held it close up to my ear.	(Raise hands to ear.)
I heard the ocean roar!	
I found a tiny little shell one day,	(One hand cupped as if holding little shell.)
Upon the ocean sand.	
The waves had worn it nice and smooth.	(Pretend to roll shell between palms of both hands.)
It felt nice in my hand.	

Day at the Beach

Ocean breeze blowing,	(Sway arms back and forth.)
Feet kick and splash,	(Kick feet.)
Ocean waves breaking	
On the rocks with a crash.	(Clap hands loudly.)
Boys finding seashells,	(Look toward ground—pick up shell.)
Girls sifting sand,	(Pretend to pick up sand—sift through fingers.)
Friends building castles As high as they can.	(Placing one hand on top of other—continue going higher.)
I stretch my arms out Far as they'll reach.	(Stretch arms out to sides.)
Oh, my what fun On this day at the beach.	

Cooking
- Boil as many shells as there are children in your group. Use them as dishes for snacks. Fill them with:

62

- Pieces of fruit
- Peanuts
- Popcorn
- Raisins

Thinking Games
- Get to Know Your Stone: Give each child a stone. Allow a few minutes for them to examine the stone thoroughly. Encourage them to look for special markings such as colors or bumps. Let them feel it all over. Have them gently touch it to their face. Some may want to smell it. Put all the stones in a box. At this point either put the box up or pass it to each person and let him find his special stone.
  Extension: If your group would like to name their stones, let them. Maybe some of the children would like to tell the group a story about their stone, what it likes to eat, how it plays, when it sleeps, and so on. When the game is finished, put the box of stones in the Manipulative Center. The children will find many ways to use them.
- Have six to eight shells or stones of different sizes in a box. Take them out so that all the children can see them. Ask them which one is the largest. Put that one to one side. Ask which is the smallest. Put that one at the opposite side. Then ask which one is the second largest. Put that next to the largest. Continue until you get to the smallest one. Now let the children look at the arrangement.

Active Games
- Walk around the Shell: Have the children get in a circle. Give each child a shell. Have him put it on the floor in front of him. Play music, have the children hold hands, and let them walk in tempo around the shells. When the music stops, have each child pick up the shell in front of him. Go around the circle and let each child tell something that would fit in his shell. Put the shell down and play again. Try it on several other days using different types of music.

Music
- Sing, "Sand and Stones and Shells." Introduce one verse a day. Sing to the tune of "Oats and Peas and Barley."
  Sand and stones and shells, my friend.
  Sand and stones and shells, my friend.
  We look at them. We play with them.
  Oh, sand and stones and shells, my friend.

Sand, it is so nice to touch.
Sand, it is so nice to touch.
Pour it, pat it, shake it, wet it.
Sand, it is so nice to touch.

Stones, they can be rough or smooth.
Stones, they can be rough or smooth.
Big or small, we like them all.
Oh, stones, they can be rough or smooth.

Shells, they come from the sea.
Shells, they come from the sea.
Pretty shells for you and me.
Oh, shells, they come from the sea.

Sand and stones and shells, my friend.
Sand and stones and shells, my friend.
We look at them, we play with them.
Oh, sand and stones and shells, my friend.
Nancy Leatzow

Room Enhancements
- Get a fish net to hang the artwork on.
- Get beach scene pictures from a travel agency, airlines, etc.
- Hang beach umbrellas from the ceiling.
- Look at the local library for an art print of a beach scene or landscape featuring cliffs or boulders.

Bibliography
Everybody Needs a Rock by Byrd Baylor
From Afar It Is an Island by Munari Bruno
Shells Are Where You Find Them by Elizabeth Clemons
Rocks by Edward Gallob
Houses from the Sea by Alice Goudey
Wonders of the World of Shells, Sea, and Freshwater by Morris Jacobsen
Stone Soup by Ann McGovern
Guess What Rocks Do by Barbara Rinkoff
Sylvester and the Magic Pebble by William Steig
A Shell Collectors Handbook by A. Verrill
Filmstrip: Stone Soup by Weston Woods
Study Prints: Common Rocks by SVE, 1964

In addition to developing a unit of activities, a teacher selects predictable objectives. To accomplish this task, Mary Alice asked

BROOKE BORTNER, AGE 11.

herself, "What do I predict that my students will learn from studying this unit?" The purpose of predictable objectives is to provide the teacher with direction and to focus on specific learning concepts. Each unit has four to six predictable objectives. Predictable objectives for the unit on sand, stones, and shells are as follows:

The child will be able to:

- manipulate various forms of sand, stones, and shells.
- identify and describe various kinds of sand, stones, and shells.
- transform sand, stones, or shells into art forms.
- develop classification systems for stone and/or shell collections.
- experience counting stones and shells from one to twenty.

Each unit will also contain unpredictable learning objectives, or learnings not predicted by the teacher. A good curriculum is replete with unpredictable objectives. Unpredictable objectives in the shell/stones/sand unit might be that the students learn the names of various stones and shells.

Patty's father collected stones. His collection was quite extensive, and he had shared his hobby with Patty. Patty brought them into class and spent many hours during individual exploration time sharing her knowledge with other children.

What the students learned from their interactions with Patty are classified as unpredictable objectives. Mary Alice was not able to predict that she would have a student with extensive information about stones. However, teachers expect and accept unpredictable objectives. Mary Alice feels that the occurrence of these experiences is her ultimate goal. She knows that a well-planned, stimulating environment invites spontaneous learning. The children's unpredictable learnings are her reward for the long hours of planning.

How Experiences Should Be Organized

Having determined what is to be learned and what experiences will be provided, the teacher proceeds to the third step of curriculum planning—*how experiences should be organized.*

Mary Alice was excited about this unit. She had spent time collecting materials and ideas. She had organized her ideas into a unit that considers both learning centers and group experiences. She knew that it was the final step in her planning that would make her ideas come alive. This last step was to place the ideas onto a daily schedule, tailoring them to her class and providing for the needs and interests of individual children.

Mary Alice teaches a full-day kindergarten program. She had devised a daily schedule that fit the need of her class and the school (see fig. 9).

As Mary Alice had worked at her kitchen table, transforming her unit into a workable lesson plan, she had experienced the excitement of the creative process. What had begun as a routine task took on an attitude of play. Her creativity and ingenuity accommodated the unit to the interests and abilities of her children.

Mary Alice's lesson plan was a blueprint. As the architect, she had built her plan brick by brick. She had considered the patterns and rhythms of learning. A careful sequencing of ideas enabled one activity to grow into the next. Her understanding of the young child's love of repetition had stimulated her to schedule the repetition of activities for optimal learning. She had planned for the introduction of fresh materials throughout the unit.

As Mary Alice became involved in her planning, she had pictured individual children. Chris would enjoy the sand experiment. Eric would be eager to learn more about stones. Melinda would assert herself as head lifeguard at the beach. As Mary Alice had imagined the children interacting with the environment, additional ideas had come to mind, and she had added them to her plan.

The following lesson plan illustrates Mary Alice's week-long schedule.

LESSON PLAN

Objectives
1 Manipulating
2 Verbalizing
3 Transforming
4 Classifying
5 Counting

Theme: Sand, Stones, Shells   Dates: May 2-6

	Monday	Tuesday	Wednesday	Thursday	Friday
9:00 Outside	Add miniature toys to sand area—cars, trucks, people.	Add water to area. Provide pitchers for pouring.	Continue sand play with water and miniature toys. (If rainy, set up outside activities at sand/water table.)	Bring water table outside and scrub stones and shells.	Add sand combs. Make patterns. Check sand experiment.
9:30 Group Time	Introduce: Ocean Shell. Give each child a shell. Explore it: smell, feel, see, hear. Have several children tell about their shell.	Ocean Shell Introduce: Day at the Beach. Discuss shells. Play Walk around the Shell.	Ocean Shell Day at the Beach Let each child examine a rock. Encourage them to name their rocks. Play Pass the Rock.	Ocean Shell Day at the Beach Set up sand experiment by measuring and pouring water into different types of sand. Put near window. Watch all day.	Ocean Shell Day at the Beach Categorize stones and shells.
Individualizing	Chris: Ask Chris about his shell. Needs language helps.	Greg: Needs coordination.	Catherine: Needs finger exercise.	Chris: Self-concept. Let him carry sand experiment to window.	Eric: Needs to talk.
9:50 Independent Exploration	Have children help hang the fish net near the art area.	Have children help hang umbrellas.	Make books with those who want. Have them bring their rocks with them.	Watch sand experiment.	Boil shells so they will be sanitized by snack time.
Individualizing	Chris: Real interest in shells.	Greg: Work with him in large muscle.	Derrick: Likes to write.	Catherine: Work with art.	Derrick: Encourage more categorizing.
Blocks	Put stones and shells in area.	Tape butcher paper to floor.	Encourage children to build reefs, etc.	Continue	Continue
Art	Stone sculpture	Glue designs	Glue designs	Collage shells	Collage stones, shells, sand on meat tray.

Evaluation

	1	2	3	4	5
Derrick					
Melinda					
Chris					
Eric					
Greg					
Carin					
Catherine					
Susan					
Bob					
Jeff					

	Monday	Tuesday	Wednesday	Thursday	Friday	Evaluation
Science	Display sand, stones, shells with pans for sorting.	Add magnifying glass.	Continue	Encourage children to sort stones and shells.		
Dramatic Play	Set up beach.		Add lifeguard chair.	Add picnic basket and blanket.		
Large Muscle	Outside					
Language	Slides of beach books available	Tape book Everybody Needs a Rock.	Continue slides.	Take time to read books to interested children.	Show filmstrip of stones and shells again.	
Manipulative	Shakers	Stone sorting	Stone counting			
11:45 Group Time	Introduce: Sand, Stones, and Shells to the tune of "Oats, Peas, Barley."	Sing Sand, Stones, and Shells—two verses.	Sing Sand, Stones, and Shells—three verses. Add movements.	Sing Sand, Stones, and Shells—four verses with movements.	Sing entire song. Clap as you sing, slap thighs.	
3:30 Independent Exploration—Any Special Activity	Introduce easel painting. Have paper cut in shape of shells.	Paint butcher paper taped in morning.	Play categorizing game with children.	Do stone painting.	Talk about art print on wall. Have children make up stories about it.	
4:15 Group Time	Read Sylvester and the Magic Pebble.	Read Everybody Needs a Rock. Have children hold a rock.	Read Stone Soup.	Have filmstrip of stones and shells. Check sand experiment.		
4:30 Quiet Free Time—Any Special Activity	Whisper song Sand, Stones, and Shells. Say: Ocean Shell.	Listen to the tape Everybody Needs a Rock.	Talk about poster on wall. Describe what is going on in the picture.	Discuss sand experiment.	Enjoy all the fingerplays and songs. Read any stories that the children wrote during the week.	
Individualizing	Melinda: Needs to practice whispering.	Eric, Melinda, Carin need work on memory.	Eric, Chris need language helps.	Eric: Self-concept—let him report about sand.	Let young authors read their own books.	
5:00 End-of-Day Activity	Share one thing each child enjoyed during that day.	Talk about art activity they are taking home.	Tomorrow they will see a filmstrip.	Today we added a picnic basket to the beach—what is in the basket?	On Monday we will begin a unit about machines. What will the children do over the weekend?	

6:00- 8:00	Quiet independent exploration
8:00- 8:30	Bathroom
8:30- 9:00	Eat breakfast
9:00- 9:30	Outside
9:30- 9:50	Group time
9:50-10:45	Independent exploration
10:45-11:15	Clean up and wash for lunch
11:15-11:45	Lunch
11:45-12:30	Group time
12:30- 3:00	Nap
3:00- 3:30	Wake up and bathroom and snack
3:30- 4:00	Independent exploration
4:00- 4:15	Clean up
4:15- 4:30	Group time
4:30- 5:00	Quiet independent exploration
5:00-----	End-of-the-day activity

Fig. 9. Daily Schedule

How Student Learning Will Be Evaluated

The final step of curriculum planning is to determine *how student learning will be evaluated*. When Mary Alice had completed her lesson plan, she had reviewed the predictable objectives for the unit. She knows that objectives and evaluation are closely aligned. Predictable objectives determine what elements of the learning experience will be assessed. When objectives are changed, evaluation is also changed. Mary Alice may use the same unit next year but may change the objectives and evaluation to correspond more closely with a specific group of children.

Mary Alice decided to evaluate each student's progress according to the following criteria, which correspond to her predictable objectives. She would observe each child:

- Manipulating. Did student manipulate various forms of sand, stones, shells?
- Verbalizing. Was student able to identify and describe various kinds of sand, stones, and shells in the classroom?
- Transforming. Did student use art process to develop an art form?
- Classifying. Did student classify stones and/or shells into identifiable categories?
- Counting. Did student count stones or shells correctly to twenty?

As she waited for her class to arrive on their first day of this new unit, Mary Alice listed each child in her class in the evaluation

CHRISTOPHER LEATZOW, AGE 11.

space of the lesson plan. She boxed five spaces after each child's name—a space for each evaluation criteria. At completion of the unit she would be able to check each objective met by the child.

The conclusion of a teaching unit does not necessitate the termination of favorite activities. In fact, Mary Alice's children enjoyed this unit so much that she has decided to extend it into her unit on machines. After all, stones can be lifted by levers, and baskets of shells can be transported by pulleys. Mary Alice looks forward to building on her children's knowledge by adding this unexpected element to the new unit.

Seven

The Child's
World

Mark glances toward the block center just as three-year-old Frank grabs a block out of Carma's hand and pushes her backward. Mark moves toward Frank and corrects him in an angry voice. He is surprised to see Frank dissolve into a flood of tears. Mark knows he spoke harshly but he does not feel that he provoked such an extreme response.

If Mark could understand Frank's point of view, he would see the logic of Frank's behavior. Frank adores Mark. Mark is not only Frank's first teacher but also his primary role model. Earlier in the morning Mark said, "Now, Frank, when you finish playing with these blocks, I want you to put them all back on the shelf." Frank remembered this directive. It was important to him to show Mark that he could put the blocks away himself. This desire to please was so important to Frank that when Carma sat down to help, he viewed her as interfering with the job that he was doing for Mark. Thus, impulsively, he grabbed the block from Carma and pushed her.

Frank's response no longer appears extreme. He took the block from Carma in order to put it away himself and please Mark. Instead, this very act provoked Mark's disapproval. It was more than Frank could bear.

In the ego-centered world of the young child, words and thoughts have almost magical powers. In the situation described above, Frank was not only hurt by the way Mark spoke to him, but he was also disappointed with Mark for not understanding the situation. Frank had worked hard to do exactly as Mark had instructed. Mark should have known that.

Piaget's extensive research has shown that children think very differently from adults. They live in a world where everything is exactly as it appears to be. For instance, a child may count six objects and state that there are six. However, when the objects are moved, the young child will need to count again. They look different; therefore, they are different. Only time and experience enable the child to construct an understanding of number conservation (six is always six, no matter how it is arranged).

A further study of Piaget's findings reveals the primary achievements of the preoperational child (ages two through eight) to be a mastery of conservation, classification, seriation, and the symbolic function. The preoperational child begins to utilize language, to dream, and to engage in dramatic play. This discovery of language leads to a strong belief in its power. On Halloween, Danny, dressed as Superman, becomes distressed. "Teacher, tell them to stop calling me Superman. I'm not Superman. I'm Danny." Words are powerful to Danny. If the children continue to name him Superman, maybe he will really become Superman. This is a frightening prospect for a four-year-old boy who relies on significant adults to care for him.

There is much to learn from Piaget's work, as well as from current research in the cognitive development of children. Teachers need to be familiar with studies of development in order to understand and deal respectfully with the young child. Yet, it is also important to realize that while young children think very differently from adults, they share the same feelings. "Children are most like us in their feelings and least like us in their thoughts" (Elkind 1981, p. 187).

The child's world is characterized by a tremendous effort to understand and make sense of conflicting adult demands, a vast and sometimes scary world, and his own confusing feelings and thoughts. The teacher provides trust and support, which helps the child to figure out the world and his place in it. She creates and maintains the environment of discipline.

The environment of discipline assists the young child to develop autonomy, purpose, and competence. He feels good about himself and begins to consider the needs of others. He enjoys his positive interactions with peers and teachers, which reinforce the good feelings about himself. He explores and learns about the world around him. His explorations are sometimes carried out alone, at other times in cooperation with friends. These positive learning experiences extend his ability to interact with and to solve problems with peers, and these accomplishments enable him to like himself more and to engage in unlimited discoveries.

These personal, social, and physical elements of the environment work together to encourage each child's growth; but it is the teacher who creates the environment. It is the teacher who understands the world of the child and who creates this joyous and creative environment where the child delights, discovers, and learns to control his impulses.

CARIN PANKROS, AGE 5.

Chapter 7, "The World of the Child," examines ways in which the teacher disciplines or instructs the child to feel good about himself, to work and play cooperatively with others, and to make sense of an often confusing world. According to Selma Fraiberg (1959, p. 146), ". . . social development, the acquisition of standards of behavior, the restriction of impulses and urges, will not develop without teaching. The little child will not acquire control over his impulses unless we require him to." Early childhood educators work gently and patiently to help young children develop socially and acquire self-control. "We are teachers. We hold up standards to the child, often a little beyond what he can actually achieve, but we know how difficult this learning is and we accept the lapses, the regressions, and the plateaus when they inevitably occur" (Fraiberg 1959, p. 158).

Over time, the teacher instructs each child in the art of self-discipline. She does this by modeling, supporting, and correcting.

The Teacher Models

Children model much of their behavior and attitudes from significant adults. Bandura's research indicates that children model their behavior after their teacher. Teachers who yell tend to have loud classes, and, not surprisingly, quiet teachers usually have quiet classes. From this it follows that when children become too loud, an advisable strategy is for the teacher to lower her voice (Osborn and Osborn 1981).

Every teacher needs to ask herself, "What behaviors and attitudes do I want to model for my children?" When teachers value creativity, children tend to be creative; teachers who value cooperation have cooperative children; and if teachers don't care, their children usually don't care.

Teachers promote the growth of self-discipline by modeling trust, respect, positive behavior, self-control, honest feelings, and an enjoyment of life.

Trust

Trust is not only the first stage of psychosocial development, but it is also the foundation of every human relationship. Early childhood educators realize that, before a meaningful relationship can develop with a child, trust must be established. Chapter 10, "Creative Problem Solving," describes how teachers demonstrate trust by being interested in each child, by expressing a willingness to listen, by reacting nonjudgmentally, and by using appropriate body language.

Sensitive teachers work at maintaining each child's trust. Trustworthy behavior includes keeping promises and honestly acknowledging mistakes.

Cheryl stood outside the classroom door, stamping her feet and saying, "No, you keep the book." Mrs. Romero could not understand why this usually cooperative child was being so obstinate. Cheryl's mother wanted her to bring a new picture book to school, but Cheryl refused. Mrs. Romero had no idea that Cheryl's refusal stemmed from two past experiences with bringing books into the classroom. Each time Mrs. Romero had promised to read the book to Cheryl, and each time she forgot that promise during the course of a busy day. Cheryl felt betrayed and didn't want to bring another book to school.

Mrs. Romero had demonstrated that teachers are not to be trusted. If most of Cheryl's experiences at school are positive, her disappointment in her teacher may eventually be forgotten; but if Mrs. Romero consistently neglects to follow through on her promises, Cheryl may become uncooperative or may develop into a "behavior problem."

Because Mrs. Romero is a sensitive teacher, though sometimes caught up with the activities of the day, Cheryl's behavior in this case triggered the memory of unkept promises. Mrs. Romero walked toward Cheryl, stooped down, and, placing a hand on her shoulder, said, "Cheryl, you are afraid that if you bring your book inside, I will be too busy to read it to you. I'm sorry that I didn't read your other books. I made a mistake. Everybody makes mistakes sometimes. Could we sit together in the cozy corner and read part of this book?"

Mrs. Romero was able to correct her past mistake. In doing so, she modeled honest and trusting behavior. The next time Cheryl makes a mistake she will be better able to accept it because "everybody makes mistakes"—even her teacher!

Respect

Everyone wants to be treated with respect. Children learn respect toward others if adults treat them with dignity. Teachers who understand child development are able to respect children as they really are. When four-year-olds engage in "bathroom" talk, the realistic teacher either ignores what she perceives to be typical four-year-old behavior, or she may take the child aside and say, "Most people don't like to hear those words. If you need to say them, go into the bathroom and shut the door so we can't hear you."

When Brendon began to preface every sentence with "Jesus!" his teacher quietly explained to him who Jesus was and why many people love him. She also explained that it makes some people feel bad to hear Jesus' name used like that. Brendon's swearing stopped. His subtle request for information had been respectfully granted.

When teachers treat children with respect, children feel good about themselves and behave respectfully toward others. When Mrs. Allen sat on the floor in total exhaustion and said, "I don't know what I am going to do with you children today," five-year-old Martha, looking concerned, said, "You're having a bad day. You're tired. I know how you feel." Mrs. Allen laughed. Yes, Martha really did know how she felt. Martha often became overly tired at school, and her words were the very words her teacher had so often spoken to her.

Positive Behavior

Developing a positive attitude in order to provide a model of positive behavior can be a challenge. Much of society is geared toward negativism—from the daily news, which reports what is wrong in the world, to daily contacts with loved ones, who often find it easier to criticize than support. Positive behavior includes positive language and an ability to turn negative situations into opportunities for growth.

Lillian Katz (1977, p. 115) has expressed her concern over a type of teacher behavior she has observed in early childhood centers throughout the country. She calls it the "Nobody's Home Phenomenon." This phenomenon involves teachers who smile, praise, pat children on the head, and employ words like "nice," "good," and "pretty." This teacher behavior makes Dr. Katz uncomfortable. The smile seems hollow. The words have no meaning. There are no realistic connections with individual children. This supposedly positive behavior is, in fact, unsupportive of children's growth. These teachers are modeling superficiality and intellectual dullness. It is as if "nobody's home."

As director of an early childhood center, Arlene Bicknell reminds her teachers every year that her rule for teachers is, "You may not say 'Don't,' 'No,' or 'Stop.' " Arlene is not permissive. She knows children need limits, but she feels that limits need to be communicated positively. The teacher's challenge is to discover alternatives to negative statements. She quotes an old study by Wylie (1930), which found that 74 percent of preschool children complied with positive statements and resisted negative ones (Phyfe-Perkins 1981).

Because Arlene's rule is clear, Melanie made it her goal for the school year to eliminate negative statements from her speech. She learned to replace:

"Don't run" with "Walking is safe."

"Stop yelling" with "Quiet voices inside."

"Don't do that" with "You need to find a better way."

Melanie worked hard and felt that she accomplished her goal. Yet, over the summer, she found herself slipping back into old patterns of negative phrasing. Melanie knows that she will always need to work at being a positive person, and she enjoys the challenge.

Chapter 9, "Creativity," describes children gluing paper to the wall. Rather than reprimanding them for inappropriate behavior, their teacher assumes that they want to be constructive rather than destructive. She observes their behavior for several minutes before saying, "It looks as if you would like to wallpaper this wall. That's a good idea, but we need to prepare the wall first." The children help her to wash the glue off the wall and tack up butcher paper. Because of a teacher's positive approach and personal creativity, these children were able to feel good about themselves and work cooperatively at a constructive activity.

Self-Control

"Several studies have found a high correlation between punitive parents and aggressiveness on the part of the child. . . . Studies also suggest that where parents lack sufficient self-control, the child often lacks self-control" (Osborn and Osborn 1981, pp. 62, 63).

Teachers committed to helping children become self-disciplined persons—persons who will eventually control themselves, their feelings, and their lives—model self-control. When teachers yell and punish, they should not be surprised by children who yell and fight.

Honest Feelings

However, teachers are human beings with limited patience. Modeling honest feelings can have a positive effect on children. The key to an open expression of feelings is to focus on the feeling. When a teacher says, "I'm feeling crabby today. I didn't sleep well last night. You will need to be patient with me," she enlists the class's cooperation. She warns them of external factors influencing her behavior. And she extends an invitation to them to be as thoughtful of her as she usually is of them.

When a child does push a teacher past her limits, she expresses honest anger in a supportive manner by focusing on her feelings and the child's behavior rather than on the child himself. The following statement focuses on the child: "I've told you for the last time to stop bothering Jake. What's the matter with you, anyway? I've had it with you." The same situation could be handled by focusing on feelings and behaviors: "I feel angry when you bother Jake. I am upset. Interfering with another person's work is not acceptable in this classroom."

When teachers describe their feelings they confront the problem in a nonthreatening manner and enable the child to participate in the solution. This approach also gives children permission to express their own feelings. The teacher in the last example was pleased to hear Jake, a quiet child, say, "Quit bothering me."

Enjoyment of Life

Finally, when teachers model an enjoyment of life, their children are able to enjoy living and learning. Teachers need to share their interests and delights with children. What child can resist his teacher's very favorite story when read with enthusiasm and conviction? Teachers who love nature have children who are eager to learn about the natural world. When teachers enjoy cooking, children love to cook. (Sean's mother was surprised to learn that the pancakes he loved at school were made from the same ingredients as the pancakes he refused to eat at home!)

A teacher's enjoyment of life is the glue that holds everything together. Careful planning of the environment and curriculum, an understanding of human development, and effective communication skills add depth to the classroom when combined with a sense of enjoyment and delight.

78

BROOKE BORTNER, AGE 11.

The Teacher Supports

Early childhood educators are aware of the difficulties as well as the joys of childhood. They know that young children want to have friends, to cooperate with supportive adults, and to make sense of the world in which they live. Teachers work hard at supporting the child's ability to balance autonomy with cooperation and to develop a positive self-concept as well as respect for others. Teachers support the young child's ability to behave appropriately and to exercise self-discipline through warmth, awareness of child development, preparation of the physical environment and curriculum, clear expectations and limits, rules with reasons, clear instructions, physical and mental presence, plans designed to ease transitions, encouragement and compliments, and the attitude of looking at acts rather than words.

Warmth

Educators have long known that children need adult-imposed limits in order to develop self-control. Discipline that is either extremely lenient or extremely harsh produces the same result: a child who has not had the opportunity to develop internal controls (Fraiberg 1959).

Chapter 9 describes the creative atmosphere that is neither authoritarian nor permissive. It states that the teacher determines limits that support and guide. Osborn and Osborn (1981) add a new dimension to the authoritarian/permissive continuum. Their dimension is the continuum of warmth/hostility.

Osborn and Osborn had always viewed freedom as a positive factor in child-rearing. However, when they interviewed adults reared in free and permissive environments, they found them to be "uncertain, listless, and even hostile." Further investigation led to the discovery that what appears to be freedom is often a lack of concern. Parents who allow children to do whatever they want and teachers with "anything goes" attitudes are not being free with children. They are being irresponsible and uncaring.

The warmth/hostility continuum evaluates the emotional climate. Children are able to deal positively with greater amounts of authoritarian control or permissiveness when it is communicated with love and warmth. Conversely, even optimal limits can be harmful to a child's development when administered with coldness and hostility.

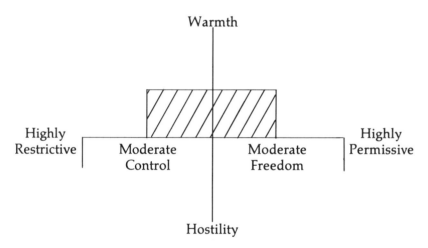

Fig. 10. Environmental Continuum
Reprinted with permission of authors. Reproduced from: Osborn, D. K., and Osborn, J. D. Discipline and classroom management. Education Associates, P.O. Box 8021, Athens, GA 30601.

Figure 10 illustrates the area of optimal development. Figure 11 lists the qualities that characterize children's behavior in each of the four following categories:
- Warm/Restrictive
- Warm/Permissive

80

- Hostile/Restrictive
- Hostile/Permissive

Figure 11 illustrates the harmful effects on children of a cold, hostile, or uncaring environment. Both warm/restrictive and warm/permissive environments produce positive attributes in children. Children who are socialized by warm-restrictive adults are polite, obedient, compliant, and minimally aggressive, but they tend to be submissive, dependent, and lacking in creativity. Children socialized by warm-permissive adults are friendly, outgoing, independent, creative, and minimally aggressive. Osborn and Osborn illustrate the area of optimal development as extending equally toward the restrictive and permissive extremes. Because the environment of discipline leads to the development of autonomy, purpose, creativity, and self-discipline, it extends further toward the permissive extreme of the continuum. Figure 12 illustrates the environment of discipline.

Osborn and Osborn (1981, p. 37) conclude that "the key question is not one of control—rather it is one of love and understanding."

	Restrictive	Permissive
Warm	Submissive Dependent Polite Neat Obedient Minimally aggressive Not creative Maximally compliant	Socially outgoing Creative Independent Friendly Problem solving Minimally aggressive

Hostile	Evidence of neurotic
	  problems
	More quarreling and
	  shyness with peers
	Delinquent behavior
	Socially withdrawn
	Maximally aggressive
		Noncompliant
		Maximally aggressive
		Some delinquent behavior
		Evidence of neurotic
		  problems
		Hedonistic behavior
		Self-centered

Fig. 11. Characteristics of Children's Behavior
Reprinted with permission of author. From an unpublished manuscript by D. K. Osborn.

Awareness of Child Development

An understanding of Erikson's stages of psychosocial growth gives the teacher added insight, which enhances her sensitivity and

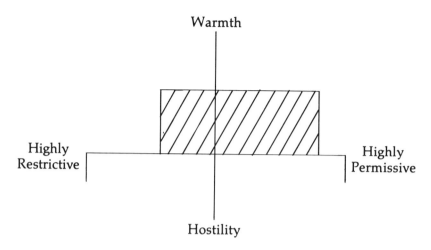

Fig. 12. The Environment of Discipline Continuum

effectiveness. The teacher who views trust as the basis of human growth and interaction builds trust into the classroom environment. When teachers understand the young child's struggle to become autonomous and self-controlled, they accept certain oppositional behaviors (see the section, "Looking at Acts, Not Words") and they provide opportunities for children to make choices and act independently. The supportive teacher knows that achieving a sense of purpose through the exercise of initiative is the crowning achievement of the preschool years, and she systematically supports this achievement through her room arrangement, curriculum, and personal support. Children with a sense of purpose move into the period of industry and competence. Early childhood educators respect the young child's work and play, and they appreciate his ability to take initiative, to become involved, and to demonstrate competence.

The greater the teacher's understanding of each child's developmental level and point of view, the greater will be her ability to identify with that child, to provide meaningful experiences, and to support his growth toward a self-disciplined personhood.

Preparation of the Physical Environment and Curriculum

When discipline is viewed as instruction, its emphasis shifts from correction to prevention. The key elements of preventive discipline are careful preparation of the physical environment and a rich and stimulating curriculum. The importance of these elements can easily be overlooked in a classroom where they are present. Their absence dramatically argues their case. When an appropriate room arrangement and interesting curriculum are absent, teachers spend much of their time "disciplining" bored and confused children. When the physical environment invites creative involvement, children are free to learn and teachers are free to teach.

Clear Expectations and Limits

In her review of the literature Bowermaster notes that Anderson, Evertson, and Emmer (1979) found that

the more effective teachers were those who had clear notions of acceptable student behaviors and fashioned their classroom structure so as to actively discourage intolerable behaviors. In contrast, the less effective managers did not seem to have clearly formed ideas of what student's behaviors should look like and often waited until after problems developed before talking to the students about expected behaviors. [Bowermaster 1981, p. 3]

This research demonstrates that children are only able to conform to a standard of behavior when a standard exists.

Nick Tosca wants his children in nursery school to be free, creative, and uninhibited. He loves being with the children and runs a well-planned classroom rich in unusual materials for the children to explore. His students are artistic, inventive, and involved in their dramatic play. However, his group times are confusing and frustrating. Nick's problems stem from his expectations. Because he expects individual expression, his students are expressive. However, because he has not clearly defined his own limits for the children, they have not learned to listen, cooperate, or wait for their turn in a group situation. Nick becomes concerned.

He gradually develops a clear sense that he needs to support his children's ability to function as part of a group of people—to be cooperative and thoughtful. He shortens his group times to be more appropriate for young children and develops strategies that encourage cooperative behaviors. Nick notices small improvements, but it is not until the next year that he sees a definite change. He begins the new school year with clear expectations for student behavior, and his students respond accordingly.

As Nick prepares himself for his second year of teaching, he takes time to consider his own limits. His most frustrating times as a teacher occur when he allows the children to exceed his own tolerance levels. He analyzes these tolerance levels in order to establish clear expectations for the coming school year. The following chart (fig. 13) helped Nick to evaluate his feelings about noise, activity, mess, oppositional behavior, disagreements, and flexibility.

Nick knows that he has a high tolerance for noise and activity, but he is surprised to realize that he has a low tolerance for mess.

	High	Medium	Low
Noise	√		
Activity	√		
Mess			√
Oppositional Behavior		√	
Disagreements		√	

Fig. 13. Assessment of Teacher Tolerance Levels

This realization helps him to articulate clear rules, "Before you begin a new activity, you need to put away the materials you are through with." Nick also realizes that, while he views himself as child-centered, he is only moderately accepting of oppositional behavior and arguments. He knows he needs to grow in his ability to help children work out their own problems in a constructive manner (see chapter 10).

Once Nick understands his own limits, he is able to define clear expectations of acceptable behavior for the children. He is also able to communicate his expectations verbally and nonverbally.

Rules wi:h Reasons

Young children need clear rules that make sense. Children who understand the rules are able to work at compliance. According to Bowermaster (1981, p. 5) Emmer, Evertson, and Anderson (1979) found that clearly stated rules "may actually serve to reduce anxiety about behaving correctly by helping students know what to expect and what is expected of them."

When rules make sense, children are more willing to comply, even when their teacher is not watching. Children who understand the reasons for rules internalize the reasons as well as the behaviors. Rules with reasons support the development of conscience.

Brophy and Evertson (1976) found that the more effective teachers have few rules that are general and flexible. These few rules are clearly stated but may be adapted to fit the situation (Bowermaster 1981). Many early childhood educators effectively operate their classroom on one general rule—"You may not hurt yourself or anyone else." While this statement is negative, it is clear, and children understand it. This rule is easy to remember and applies to all undesirable behavior.

When Marcie hits Suzanne, her teacher says, "Hitting hurts. You may not hurt Suzanne, and I won't let Suzanne hurt you."

As Marcello runs across the room, his teacher moves next to him and, reaching out to stop him, says, "Last year a boy ran here. He fell and hurt himself. I don't want you to be hurt. Walking is safe."

After Roman was fitted for glasses, some of the children began to call him "four-eyes" and "funny face." Their teacher said, "Calling Roman names hurts his feelings. You cannot hurt Roman's feelings, and I won't let anyone hurt yours."

Jean is angry and begins to break crayons. Her teacher stops the destructive behavior by holding Jean's hands and says, "Jean, if you break our crayons, we won't be able to draw pictures with them. We will all be hurt by this. We need to take care of our supplies. I'll help you put the crayons away. Then let's take a walk together."

It is necessary here to point out the difference between intentional and accidental destruction of equipment. If a child is deliberately destroying an item, this hurtful behavior must be stopped. It may actually be a child's way of asking for help. However, when a child accidentally breaks supplies or equipment, he needs to be reassured. A teacher may say, "I know it was an accident. Everybody makes mistakes. Just last week I broke one of my favorite plates."

When the reasons for rules are explained, children understand their necessity and are internally motivated to comply. Rules that are clear, general, and flexible help children to develop self-discipline.

Clear Instructions

Even excellent teachers make the mistake of stating what is wrong without suggesting acceptable actions. Supportive teachers work at giving instructions or suggestions that are clear.

Instead of saying, "Stop fighting," say, "Hitting hurts. We need to talk about this."

Instead of saying, "You're up too high," say, "I am uncomfortable when you are up there. You need to come down."

Instead of saying, "This table is a mess," say, "Shelly, please pass the basket so that everyone can throw away his dirty cup and napkin."

Children may want to stop fighting but need help to do so. They may infer from the statements, "You're up too high," or "This is a mess," that the teacher isn't happy about it, but it may not occur to them that teacher wants action.

Physical and Mental Presence

Teachers support self-discipline in children through their physical and mental presence. Effective teachers position themselves so that they can observe the entire room. Anderson, Evertson, and Brophy (1979) found that this type of monitoring produces higher student achievement in the elementary classroom (Bowermaster 1981).

In the early childhood classroom, children are aware of their teacher's presence, which helps them to exercise self-control and to achieve a higher degree of involvement. Whenever a teacher engages in a small-group activity, she sits so that she can continue to oversee the classroom. In this way she practices what Kounin (1970) calls "overlapping" or an ability to handle two issues simultaneously.

Mrs. Rutledge is seated on the floor in the block center engaging in sociodramatic play with three children. Her back is to the wall, and she periodically scans the room. When Rosa begins to throw play dough, Mrs. Rutledge quietly says, "Rosa, come here. I need to speak with you." She then deals with the play dough issue without interrupting the dramatic play. She has successfully demonstrated overlapping.

Teachers who position themselves effectively and move around the room support positive behavior. Brophy and Evertson (1976) report that children's disruptive behavior is "correlated positively with the likelihood of not being seen by the teacher" (Bowermaster 1981, p. 14).

Kounin (1970) also describes a teacher behavior as "with-it-ness." "With-it-ness" involves the teacher's communicating to children that she knows what is going on. Teachers who do not demonstrate "with-it-ness" make such mistakes as selecting the wrong child for correction, overlooking serious misbehaviors while handling minor violations, or letting an unacceptable behavior continue until it is "out of hand."

Early childhood educators support each child's ability to exercise self-discipline by being physically and mentally present, by demonstrating "with-it-ness" and "overlapping," and by taking an active role in children's play. Children respond positively to a warm and caring teacher who communicates interest and involvement. In her review of the research Phyfe-Perkins states, "Perkins (1980) found that the antisocial behavior of children was significantly higher in the day-care center characterized by predominantly uninvolved and directive adults" (Phyfe-Perkins 1981, p. 22).

Planning for Transitions

Teachers sometimes neglect to plan for a most important time of the day—transitions. According to Phyfe-Perkins (1981), Berk (1976) found that 20 to 35 percent of the preschool day is spent in transition. Transitions are those times when children move from one activity to another, such as from independent exploration to a group time or from snack to outdoor play. Two guidelines are essential for supporting children through smooth transitions. First, advance warning should be provided, such as, "In five minutes we need to put everything away and clean up the room," or "You need to finish that up in the next few minutes as we will be having our snack." Teachers invest time and effort into preparing an environment where children become intensely involved. It follows that they will respect this involvement by preparing the child for what comes next. This verbal alert allows the child to ease out of what he is doing.

The second guideline is to turn transition times into learning experiences. Age-old techniques such as the following one slow down the transition and move children gradually rather than as a group. This method encourages children to become more aware and observant.

"If you are wearing red, you may get your coat. If you are wearing blue . . ."

"If you have a square on your clothes, walk to the snack table. If you have a circle . . ."

"When I touch your head, quietly fly to the rug area like a gentle baby bird. Quietly hop to the rug like a fuzzy baby bunny . . ."

Additional suggestions are in the appendix.

Encouragement and Compliments

Children need realistic encouragement and specific compliments from their teachers. Such comments as, "You are having a hard time with that. But you are sticking to it. What determination!" or "What an efficient system—you hand the blocks to Jim, and he builds the road. Keep up the good work!" offer realistic encouragement. Statements like, "What an interesting painting—I see you used a wet brush here, and a dry brush here," or "I like the way you each gave Michael a piece of play dough; you are very thoughtful," focus on the work or the behavior. They expand the child's awareness of what he has accomplished and help him to feel competent.

According to Phyfe-Perkins (1981, p. 4), Stallings (1975) concluded that praise should be used "sparingly and specifically." When teachers help children to feel good about their work, children view the work and the corresponding feelings of success as the reward. Children enjoy this internal sense of competence.

Mrs. Polarski expressed a concern shared by other teachers when she said, "My children seem to be 'praise junkies.' They aren't satisfied unless they receive praise for everything they do."

Teachers avoid the "nobody's home" approach of saying, "How pretty," or "That's nice," by being specific in their comments. They support each child's ability to find satisfaction in his work rather than in adult praise.

Looking at Acts, Not Words

When early childhood educators remember that the assertion of autonomy from adult control is a primary accomplishment of the preschool years, they are not surprised or offended by oppositional behavior. This period generally begins at eighteen months and may last through age five.

The preschool child may refuse to comply with an adult's request or suggestion, not because she or he does not like the suggestion, but because of the strong need to assert autonomy. The young child may refuse a well-meaning adult's offer of help because "I want to do it myself." The struggle for autonomy and independent mastery of the world is at the heart of much oppositional behavior. [Haswell, Hock, and Wenar 1982, p. 14]

A positive resolution of the autonomy-doubt conflict provides the self-control which enables the child to develop initiative and competence in middle childhood. The sensitive teacher supports the young child through this challenge by looking at actions, not words.

During this period children often respond negatively while actually complying with an adult request. Tony says, "No, I won't put the toys away," as he begins to place them on the shelf. Responding to her teacher's suggestion that she zip her own coat, Donna states, "I won't," as she reaches down to try. In these instances the teacher stands back and observes. She accepts the child's need to express opposition while conforming in his behavior.

Alex's mother needs to take a full-time job, and she enrolls Alex at the Village Day-Care Center. Alex refuses to go. During his first day at school he announces, "I hate it here, and you can't make me like it." His teacher, Aileen, replies, "You're right. I can't make you like it. You have to be here, even though you don't want to be, but no one can make you like it. That is up to you."

Alex remains aloof for several weeks, looking things over and working out his feelings. Aileen suggests activities he might want to try. She learns from his mother where his interests lie and sets up activities to entice him. But she respects his feelings, making comments like, "You might want to see if you can figure out how the

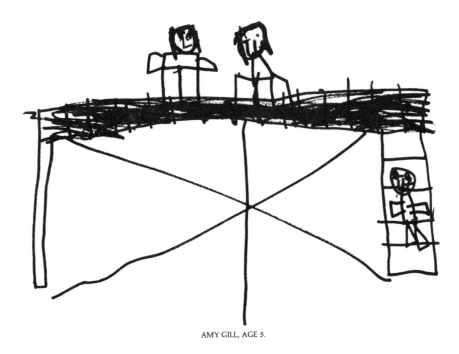

AMY GILL, AGE 5.

water wheel works," or "I know you don't want to be here; but since you need to stay until 5:00, there are some dinosaur books for you to look at." Gradually, Alex begins to enter into the workings of the center, exploring the environment and making friends. He frequently and emphatically tells Aileen that he still doesn't like school. She never tries to tell him that he should, but lovingly and respectfully she supports his attempt to accept a difficult situation.

After several months, Alex asks if he can take a particular toy home overnight. Aileen says, "You seem to like it." Alex holds two fingers about one inch apart and says, "Well, maybe this much." Aileen knows that Alex is meeting his challenge.

The Teacher Corrects

Young children are just beginning to develop self-discipline. They count on adults to help provide control. A teacher who allows a child to behave violently or inappropriately violates the child's trust. The child wants help. The preoperational child's world is filled with confusing and conflicting demands, concepts, and feelings. In attempting to understand and negotiate this barrage of information, the young child behaves impulsively. His positive impulses to love, to create, to think, and to play need to be nurtured and supported. His negative impulses to hit, to exceed appropriate limits, and to infringe on the rights of others should be firmly and lovingly corrected. The teacher corrects inappropriate behavior by looking for the reasons, offering alternatives, employing logical consequences, entering into the play, and speaking from conviction.

Looking for the Reasons

Everyone wants to feel good about himself. A person whose behavior antagonizes and alienates others cannot really like himself. Thus, the "self" and "other" concepts are unavoidably linked. A teacher corrects a child's misbehavior so that he can develop a positive self-image.

The concerned teacher is not so interested in stopping objectionable behavior as in determining the reason for the behavior. At times the reason is clear and at other times illusive. Teachers dedicated to the positive growth of each child work hard at unearthing the root of the problem. Conditions at school need to be examined in determining the possible cause.

David is somewhat quiet and cooperative as the school year begins. After several weeks his behavior changes. Each morning he walks around the room quietly disrupting other children, knocking down buildings, messing up projects, and hitting at random. His teacher works with him through gentle reprimands and discussions of rights and feelings. She even isolates him as his behavior becomes more extreme.

One morning she watches David get off the bus and push Abby into the bushes. Suddenly, she connects David's bus ride to his increasingly disruptive behavior. Checking the route, she finds that David is the first child to be picked up. His bus driver is not a teacher and expects David to be still and quiet for thirty minutes. By the time he reaches school, he is ready to explode, and he usually does!

David's empathetic teacher ignores his behavior that day but stays late after school to set up the child-sized workbench. She fastens a thick pine board into the vise and places a small saw on the bench. The next morning she greets David at the bus and tells him she has something special for him to do. She takes him to the workbench, instructs him in safety procedures, and gets him started.

Each morning David goes straight to the workbench and saws with all his might for five to ten minutes before easing into another activity. His teacher was able to correct his inappropriate and uncomfortable behavior by determining the reason and providing him with an outlet for pent-up feelings and energies.

Conditions at home also need to be considered as teachers search for the reasons behind children's behavior. While problems related to divorce, economic hardship, and "life in the fast lane" create problems for young children, the normal anxieties of growing up can sometimes be more difficult to determine. The following case study illustrates how a teacher and mother worked together to help a young girl.

Anya is four years old and seems to fit right into the nursery school setting. Her teacher, Miss Pierce, thinks of Anya as happy and self-sufficient. One day Miss Pierce notices Anya coming in from the playground with wet pants. She takes her into the bathroom to change into the spare clothes kept on hand for just such an emergency.

After several days it is evident that Anya is wetting herself daily during outside play time. Miss Pierce is concerned. She begins to take Anya to the bathroom before she goes out. She spends more time with Anya, becoming involved in her play and asking questions about her home and family, looking for clues. Finally, she confers with Anya's mother. Mrs. Wohl is aware of the problem and is a bit hostile toward a teacher who has allowed this situation to occur. Through continued discussion, Miss Pierce and Mrs. Wohl learn to trust each other and work together.

In desperation Miss Pierce discusses this situation with her former college professor, who recommends a program of behavior modification. Miss Pierce does not like the suggestion but is ready to try anything. Then Mrs. Wohl drives up—she has found the answer.

Anya's oldest brother went away to college this year. She heard him express the normal anxieties of leaving home. Then he was gone. Somehow, he left without saying good-bye to Anya, and this little girl's beloved brother was gone. She worried about him. Just as she pictured him in a scary situation beyond his control, she lost control over herself.

That weekend Matt had come home to visit. Anya's statements and questions enabled her family to understand what she had been going through. Matt assured Anya that he wanted to go to college and that he was happy. Anya was relieved. She no longer wet herself at school. Mrs. Wohl and Miss Pierce felt gratified that they had worked together. If they had not, Mrs. Wohl might not have made the connection between Anya's wetting and her concern for her brother. Miss Pierce probably would have proceeded with the behavior modification technique and viewed it as successful.

Offering Alternatives

Children's misbehavior is often most effectively corrected by offering an alternative. The better a teacher understands a child, the more effective the alternative will be. Children frequently behave unacceptably when they are frustrated, crowded, or upset about something else. The teacher who can redirect a child to an alternative activity that is personally interesting, calming, or tension-relieving usually achieves her goal—to stop the destructive behavior and to involve the child in a supportive activity that enhances his self-concept.

Leon directs his school's learning center. A concerned mother speaks to him about her son. Ardell is in kindergarten. He is active and curious and loves "bugs." His mother feels that he has been unfairly labeled a "discipline problem" when he is in actuality bored. Without making a judgment on the classroom situation, Leon assures Ardell's mother that he will try to provide Ardell with a challenge. He prepares a packet of illustrated insect books, a magnifying glass, and several mounted specimens.

When the kindergarten class comes to the learning center later that week, Ardell begins to fight with a friend. Leon puts an arm around his shoulder and leads him to the insect packet. He says, "I have something I want to show you." Leon chooses to ignore the negative behavior and focuses directly on the alternative, expressing his confidence in Ardell. Ardell returns to the learning center frequently and pursues his investigations of insect life.

When it is not possible to direct a child into an activity of specific personal interest, a teacher selects an alternative that either calms or releases tension and unsettled feelings. Calming activities include playing with water, especially feeling smooth rocks or colored gravel in warm water; molding and shaping fresh play dough; listening to quiet music or stories; taking care of a classroom pet, doll, or stuffed animal; rocking in a child-sized rocker; creating with art mediums; or taking a walk with an adult. Some activities that release tension and upset feelings are running around the playground, pounding play dough, throwing a softball or paper wad at a target, creating with art mediums, and punching a punching bag.

Carl's behavior is unacceptable. His teacher looks around the room for a quick alternative. Nothing seems right. She hands Carl a large piece of paper and tells him to tear it into as many tiny pieces as he can, then to pick up all of the pieces and place them in the collage box. By the time Carl has torn the pieces and picked them all up, he is relaxed and resumes his play. Alternatives abound for the resourceful teacher.

Employing Logical Consequences

According to social psychologist Rudolf Dreikurs (1964; Dreikurs and Gray 1968; Dreikurs and Cassel 1972), individuals who live in a democratic society need to be responsible for their own acts. When a child is disruptive, the teacher should neither ignore the behavior nor punish it.

Dreikurs recommends the use of a *logical consequence,* as opposed to punishment. This recommendation is best explained by first defining the term *natural consequence,* which occurs as a natural result of a behavior. For instance, Jesse pushes to be first on the climber. He falls down and hurts himself. Falling down is a natural consequence of pushing. Jesse was clearly responsible for both the act (pushing) and the consequence (falling and hurting). If Jesse began to push children aside in an attempt to be first on the climber and the teacher removed him and put him at the end of the line, this would be a logical consequence. While a logical consequence involves the teacher's intervention, it is always directly related to the unacceptable behavior.

When a teacher punishes, the child's awareness is focused on the punishment. The child may feel ashamed, helpless and discouraged, angry and vengeful, or happy to be receiving the teacher's attention. When a teacher arranges a logical consequence, the child sees the relationship between his behavior and the consequence of the act.

A final and important difference between a logical consequence and punishment is the attitude of the teacher.

Example 1

Cindy begins to hit. When she hits, her teacher says, "Cindy, how many times do I have to tell you not to hit? If you can't get along with the other children, you will just have to sit in this chair by yourself."

Example 2

Cindy hits Jane. The teacher moves to her side. She leads Cindy to a chair apart from the class and says, "Cindy, you have lost control of yourself. I can't let you hit. Hitting hurts. You need to sit in this chair until you are back in control and can play with your friends without hitting them."

In each example Cindy was removed and put in a chair by herself. In Example 1, Cindy's teacher publicly scolded and isolated her. In Example 2, Cindy's teacher told her privately that she needed to be alone in order to regain control. While the outcome appears the same, the teacher in Example 1 used punishment. The teacher in Example 2 used logical consequence. The child's experience and learning were different.

Entering into the Play

Supportive teachers attempt to correct inappropriate behavior without embarrassing the child or causing him to "lose face." Teachers are often able to correct a situation by entering into the child's play.

It is easier to deal positively with behavior before it crosses the line of nonacceptability. In chapter 9, "Creativity," two children are playing with trucks. As their play becomes wild, their teacher says, "Park your trucks. It's time for a coffee break." The teacher does not feel compelled to lecture them on their behavior. Her alert scanning of the classroom enables her to spot the potential trouble, enter into the play, and change its direction. She joins the "truckers," asking them about their cargo, destination, and road conditions.

Even when children's behavior is out of control, the teacher can correct it by taking a role in the play. When Chantelle Davis, who is involved in a lotto game, looks toward the dramatic play center, she sees a bitter argument taking place. Quickly, she hands her lotto card to Emily, asking her to fill in for a few minutes. She then grabs a police hat, puts it on, and enters the dramatic play. "Sergeant Davis reporting. Break it up. We've had a complaint from the neighbors." Several children find comic relief in their teacher's behavior. Others are so involved in their roles that they immediately state their complaint to "Sergeant Davis," who begins the process of creative problem solving described in chapter 10.

Speaking from Conviction

Teachers who have established a philosophy of discipline based on an understanding of human development are able to speak from conviction. When expectations and limits are clearly established in a supportive environment enriched by a creative curriculum, the teacher is free to interact with children in a warm, self-assured manner. Correction is offered firmly and confidently. Children respond positively to the corrective remarks of a teacher who means what she says.

If the teacher is uncertain, the child responds to the uncertainty rather than to the words. A firm statement reassures the child. Early childhood educators avoid the "nobody's home" phrasing of,

"Now, Susie, wouldn't you like to stop that?" when what they mean is, "That behavior is not acceptable in this classroom." Whether introducing alternatives or logical consequences or whether entering into the play, teachers need to state corrections clearly and with conviction.

Margaret Mead (1972) describes her grandmother's ability to command respect and obedience by speaking with a sense of conviction.

She meant exactly what she said, always. If you borrowed her scissors, you returned them. In like case, Mother would wail ineffectually, "Why does everyone borrow my scissors and never return them?" and Father would often utter idle threats. But Grandma never threatened. She never raised her voice. She simply commanded respect and obedience by her complete expectation that she would be obeyed. And she never gave silly orders. She became my model when, in later life, I tried to formulate a role for the modern parent who can no longer exact obedience merely by virtue of being a parent and yet must be able to get obedience when it is necessary. Grandma never said, "Do this because Grandma says so," or "because Grandma wants you to do it." She simply said, "Do it," and I knew from her tone of voice that it was necessary. [pp. 45, 46]

Conclusion

Erikson's advice (1963, p. 249) to parents is equally true for teachers. "They must be able to represent to the child a deep, and almost somatic conviction that there is meaning to what they are doing." This sense of meaning permeates the child's physical being. It is no mere intellectual exercise. The teacher's role is to provide meaning to the children's experience. She does this by modeling, supporting, and correcting.

Above all, the child seeks to make sense of the adult world and to figure out his role in it. As long as he senses a meaning to his experiences, he feels positive about himself, others, and his world.

Eight

The World of
the Teacher

The world of the teacher, like the world of the child, is character-ized by an effort to understand conflicting demands and her own confusing feelings and thoughts. The teacher's role in this world is to understand what is happening, to design a supportive environ-ment for herself, and to confront the demands of adult growth. The difference between the child's world and the teacher's world is that the teacher is the architect of her own growth as well as that of her students.

Knowledge of the adult world is gained through continual emo-tional, social, and cognitive growth. The growing teacher is aware of the world around her and the options available to her. From this knowledge she establishes priorities and makes plans.

Amy Baldwin is the director of Willowwood Day-Care Center. Every morning she arises forty-five minutes before her family to have a quiet cup of coffee, watch the early morning sun, and make plans for the day. Sometimes she writes her daily goals in a note-book. At other times, she sketches them in her mind. She plans three or four activities.

Previously, Amy had planned every minute of the day. When her schedule was not followed, she became stressful, angry, and frus-trated. Every interruption was an annoyance, because it prevented her from following her schedule. Her sense of control and con-fidence came from this organized plan.

Since following her new plan of scheduling only three or four goals, Amy feels more relaxed and has gained confidence in her ability to make realistic plans and follow through on them.

Amy also has a yearly goal. This year it is to enjoy life. Amy has been working hard, and she knows that her mental and physical health will deteriorate if she doesn't develop a more balanced life. She asks herself daily, "What will I do for enjoyment?" She doesn't feel guilty spending time on personal enjoyment because it is part of her plan. The plan gives the activity credence. Amy notices that taking time to enjoy life has made her a more positive person, and she perceives this activity as a concrete demonstration that she cares for herself. She also notices that since she has accepted the value of enjoying life, she has expanded her awareness of the world around her. She appreciates the subtle colors of the sunrise, marvels at the beauty of an egg symmetrically frying in the pan, and inhales the fragrances of life.

Just as a child needs a supportive environment to enhance his self-concept, so does the teacher. She needs to feel good about herself and to enjoy positive experiences. Chapter 7, "The World of the Child," illustrates how the teacher models, supports, and corrects in order to promote growth in self-discipline. Chapter 8, "The World of the Teacher," describes how teachers support their own growth toward becoming an inner-directed person.

The idea that adults grow and develop throughout life is discussed in the writings of Erik Erikson (1963), Carl Rogers (1962), Abraham Maslow (1962), Arthur Combs (1962), Virginia Satir (1972), and Roger Gould (1978). Their research on evolving adult personalities indicates the following characteristics of a fully functioning person—an accurate and accepting self-concept, an accurate and accepting other-concept, an enjoyment of learning, and a sense of control. These qualities are bound together by the individual's personal philosophy. As the teacher works at integrating these characteristics into her life, she supports her own development as well as that of the children. She nurtures the growth of peers and parents within the circle of support.

An Accurate and Accepting Self-Concept

The fully functioning individual feels good about herself. She sees herself as competent, likable, purposeful, and worthwhile. This sense of self is derived from interactions with others, from experiences in a nurturing world, and from the individual's own perception of her experiences.

An adequate personality is basically positive. This does not mean that life is seen as "a bowl of cherries." Rather, the positive person likes herself as she really is. Her self-concept is both accurate and accepting. In fact, it is this positive perspective that allows the healthy person to examine her negative characteristics honestly. She either accepts them as part of the human condition or works to bring about change. Like the growth process, the evolving self-concept changes throughout life. Learning to deal with change is an important skill in the process of adult development.

A healthy attitude includes the acceptance of negative characteristics. Dreikurs (1964, p. 108) calls it the "courage to be imperfect."

MELINDA NEUHAUSER, AGE 5.

Chantelle Jones is ten to fifteen pounds overweight. This fact bothered Chantelle in the past, but she has learned to accept her size as
normal for her, and she likes herself as she is. At the day-care center where she works, three-year-old Brian looks at her and says,
"Your tummy sticks out." Chantelle smiles. "You're right, Brian,
my stomach does stick out. I love to eat!" She laughs with Brian,
enjoying his honesty and appreciating his powers of observation.
Her positive self-concept accurately accepts Brian's comment.

When negative characteristics dominate an individual's experience, the resulting feelings of frustration or anguish can be turned
into the impetus for change. Elizabeth is an admired teacher. She
runs a creative and stimulating classroom and is respected by peers
and parents. However, she feels increasingly anxious about her
work. She has set her standards so high that she can never achieve
them. She sets herself up to fail. Elizabeth is so obsessed by the un-
completed tasks that she is unable to feel good about the many out-
standing achievements in her classroom.

Over Christmas break, Elizabeth decides to resign at the end of
the school year. She returns to work determined to put forth a
minimal effort. As Elizabeth lowers her expectations, she is surprised to find her interactions with the children more enjoyable.
She begins to appreciate herself as a teacher. In the past she had felt

98

CARIN PANKROS, AGE 5.

a persistent need to work harder. Her new attitude is, "I'm a good teacher, and I'm going to enjoy my last few months of teaching. Even when I don't work as hard, my children are getting a lot."

As a result of Elizabeth's desperate need to eliminate self-imposed stress, she developed more realistic standards and learned to appreciate her gift for teaching. By the end of the school year she no longer felt a necessity to resign.

An Accurate and Accepting Other-Concept

The fully functioning individual has developed a positive view of self in part through interactions with others. The self- and other-concepts develop simultaneously. When a person values herself as she really is, accepting her perceived flaws as an expression of her humanness, she is able to accept a less-than-perfect other. She feels a sense of oneness with other people. She develops empathy, compassion, and altruism. She trusts.

The teacher respects, accepts, and demonstrates faith in others by listening, accepting others' views, being nonjudgmental, and enjoying shared experiences. The feelings of caring and cherishing others are similar to the feelings of the teacher who receives a bouquet of dandelions.

Kevin walks slowly into the classroom. He holds his hands behind his back and looks around, trying to attract Miss Rhoda's attention. Finally, their eyes meet, and Kevin runs to give his teacher a handful of dandelions. He is proud of himself. He is sharing the coming of spring, the bringing of a gift of love, the positive interaction between student and teacher, and the good feelings that result from caring for another person. The child creates this joyful situation for himself and his teacher.

The feelings expressed in this teacher-child vignette are similar to the feelings shared by adults when relationships are characterized by respect, acceptance, and faith in one another.

As Sharrie stops by Lola's classroom to describe a magical moment of teaching, Lola feels the emergence of warm inner feelings. Sharrie is a first-year teacher who has had problems resolving her college ideals with the classroom reality. Other teachers had given up on Sharrie, who sometimes seemed awkward or hesitant. But Lola liked Sharrie, understood her dilemma, and had faith in her ability to resolve it. For weeks she had listened to Sharrie's concerns, helped her to clarify problems, and led her into a more realistic approach to teaching. As she listened to Sharrie describe her moment of triumph, Lola was happy that she had been able to support this vulnerable and caring person. She felt as if she had just been handed a bouquet of dandelions.

An Enjoyment of Learning

Adult growth is impelled by an ability to learn from ideas and experience. The adult who works at demonstrating self-discipline learns to attach meaning to her experiences. She sees connections between apparently unrelated ideas and events. She takes quiet time with herself to contemplate the deeper meaning of her involvements. The authentic person enjoys learning and spends time reading, attending lectures, and discussing issues with others. She thinks soundly.

Personal as well as professional growth occurs by attending professional meetings. Peter Bopki attended the annual conference of the National Association for the Education of Young Children. He was sent by his center to gather data on after-school programs. While there, he participated in workshops on computers, environmental education, and story telling. Peter returned to school with his assigned data, in addition to fresh ideas and interest in teaching. He told his children about some of his feelings and experiences at the conference. He told them stories that he had learned. The children benefited from his enthusiasm and self-renewal. They sensed the importance of Peter's trip.

DERRICK NEUHAUSER, AGE 6.

Ideas take on special meaning when they are shared with a friend. A common bond between Keyung and Alexa is their love of books. When Keyung finds a book of particular interest, she calls Alexa and says, "Alexa, you have to read this book. I need to discuss it with you." When David Elkind's book, *The Hurried Child*, was released, Keyung bought Alexa a copy. Over the next few days their telephone conversation centered on such remarks as, "Have you read what he says about sports?" or "Let's discuss schools as factories."

Sharing and exploring ideas involves teachers in a world that extends beyond the classroom. Ideas are connecting links to humanity. While ideas sometimes need to be shared, they also need to be quietly savored and digested. After reading *The Hurried Child* and discussing it with her friend, Alexa began to take long walks through the woods to contemplate Elkind's ideas. She has recently moved from the city to a country setting. She remembers the stressful feelings of fast-paced life in the city. She senses and feels the changes that are occurring within her as a result of a quieter, more simple way of life. She develops great empathy for young children who are hurried to grow up too soon. This meaningful learning experience deepens Alexa's ability to support the children in her classroom.

A Sense of Control

Just as young children work to develop a sense of autonomy within a trusting environment, adults need to feel that they are in control of themselves and their lives. When the individual senses overall self-control, she is able to work within structures determined by others. Cooperative experiences are viewed as enriching. The autonomous individual functions effectively as both leader and follower.

Since her divorce, Tricia Adams has returned to teaching. She has four children at home. The overwhelming demands of running a home and a classroom while nursing her emotional wounds have left Tricia exhausted. After several months of teaching, she begins to talk with her team teacher, Juanita. Juanita takes Tricia to the neighborhood clinic and introduces her to a counselor.

Tricia's sessions at the clinic help her to see that the most destructive aspect of her life is her complete lack of autonomy. She feels swept away by events beyond her control.

Through slow, patient, hard work, Tricia and her counselor develop a plan for enlisting the help of her children to run the home, at the same time using professional services, friends, and adult relatives for the emotional support she needs. Gradually, the children assume responsibilities at home, the teaching becomes more manageable, and Tricia begins to sense the presence of control in her life.

Tricia's second year of teaching is characterized by a beautiful expression of empathy and support for her young children. She knows how difficult it can be to develop self-discipline, to achieve a sense of control, and to live a life of dignity. She cheers and applauds her children's development of social understandings. They express cooperative and caring attitudes because of their teacher's authentic instruction.

A Personal Philosophy

The fully functioning individual has a clear personal philosophy, which serves as a guidepost for living. The teacher takes time to determine her deep beliefs. "These beliefs and values are not just intellectual or abstract ideas but, rather, deep and consistent convictions which affect actions" (Combs 1962, p. 199). This type of meaningful philosophy supports the teacher's ability to model and nurture the development of self-discipline.

A teacher needs to be clear, firm, and loving and to speak from conviction. When conviction is lacking, adults, as well as children, respond to the indecisiveness rather than the words.

An important aspect of Melissa's personal philosophy is a conviction that one needs to maintain the positive attributes of childhood. She sees creativity, play, contemplation, joy, and the need for love as positive aspects of her personality. She feels that much of her effectiveness as a teacher stems from these qualities. She perceives herself as a positive role model for her children. She also sees her meaningful relationship with each child as supporting her ability to maintain and develop these childlike qualities. This personal philosophy has enabled Melissa to act on her convictions. She believes it is the teacher's responsibility to do her best for every child in her care.

Six years ago Melissa had a student named Billy who was extremely disruptive and who frequently resorted to pushing and hitting. Generally, when Melissa worked closely with difficult students, she witnessed some sign of growth. Billy, however, remained erratic throughout the school year. In spite of the lack of improvement, Melissa never gave up on Billy. She gently stopped his hitting, provided him with alternatives, and employed logical consequences. She supported his potential to exercise self-control and conferred with his mother, offering tactful suggestions of ways to help Billy at home.

Today, as Melissa describes her problems with Billy, she speaks with confidence. Her personal commitment to her children's growth and her professional ethics had impelled her to make every effort to help this child. When she learns that he is now labeled a delinquent by many and may be experimenting with drugs, she feels sad for him. But Melissa does not think, "If only I had done more. . . ." She knows that she did everything she could have. Her behavior conformed to her personal philosophy.

The Circle of Support

As the teacher develops an accurate and accepting self- and other-concept, an enjoyment of learning, a sense of control, and a personal philosophy, she creates the environment of discipline. She models positive characteristics, supports the growth of herself and others, and corrects negative behaviors by unearthing their roots and providing for change.

The teacher who understands adult development and strives to deepen her growth toward self-discipline is able to instruct young children with authenticity and integrity. As Combs (1962, p. 212) has suggested, "Teaching is a relationship, but there can be no relationship with a non-entity."

When a developing teacher provides for her own growth, she simultaneously nurtures the growth of others. The circle of support (fig. 14) illustrates the interrelationship between the teacher's support of self, children, peers, and parents.

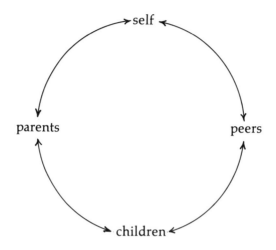

Fig. 14. The Circle of Support

The Teacher

Throughout this chapter, "The World of the Teacher," are examples of adults working to support their own growth. From Amy, who develops a more realistic system of daily planning, to Elizabeth, who learns to lower her unreasonable standards, change occurs and corrections are made. Peter sees how professional involvement enriches his teaching. Tricia struggles to gain a sense of control over her own life. Melissa's behavior conforms to her personal philosophy in times of joy as well as of challenge.

These teachers are learning to accept and appreciate themselves as they really are, to deal with necessary change, and to seek the human support that moves them toward becoming a more disciplined and authentic person.

The Child

Chapter 7, "The World of the Child," describes the teacher's role in supporting her children. She creates a rich, open-ended environment characterized by trust. She patiently instructs in the art of self-discipline.

Children show adults, by their examples of spontaneity, resiliency, and honesty, what it means to experience life to the fullest. Their fresh perspective leads the teacher toward a more spontaneous enjoyment of life. Children's egocentricity, perseverance,

104

CHRISTOPHER LEATZOW, AGE 3.

and need for adult attention quickly draw the teacher into their search for meaning.

Jason spots an ant and calls his teacher. "Teacher, teacher, come here! I got to show you somethin'!" His enthusiasm pulls her into the world of the child. Jason needs her presence to affirm his discovery. This shared experience renews a teacher's awareness of the natural world, sparks her sense of wonder, and kindles a warm, meaningful relationship.

As teachers work to provide a nurturing classroom environment, they learn to watch the children for clues. When teachers carry out inappropriate procedures, students' behaviors furnish strong clues that sometimes lead to reassessment. This process of reassessment and change show the teacher and the child in a position of mutual support. Everyone benefits as learning and growth evolve.

Heather Nemic teaches kindergarten. Intellectually, she believes in the importance of internal discipline and control; but, in setting up her classroom, she does not trust this idea and implements a system of strong external controls.

After hanging up their coats, the children are expected to sit on the circle and wait quietly until everyone arrives and Heather starts class. Heather assigns each child to a learning center and requires him to play there for twenty minutes. She sets the timer. When the timer goes off, the children rotate to the next center. If two children have a disagreement, each child is removed and sent to another center.

The next twenty minutes are taken up with bathroom time. The children wait in line in the hall and go into the bathroom two at a time. Snack is served family style with each child assigned to a table. After snack the entire class proceeds to recess. Back in the classroom, Heather conducts a music lesson and reads a story. Heather has strong control over her class.

This system of external control seems to work efficiently for a while, but Heather begins to notice children deviating from her plan, becoming irritable and unhappy. Finally, it dawns on her. The children are not developing trust, autonomy, or initiative. She is not supporting their growth in self-discipline. The children are spending their energies trying to please their teacher, a process antithetical to Heather's philosophy.

Slowly, she changes the daily schedule and allows the children opportunities to make decisions. As Heather changes the classroom environment, she changes. She feels less stress because she is no longer totally responsible for the children's behavior. Her efforts are supported by the physical environment, the curriculum, and the children themselves. Both teacher and child participate in the decision-making process. Everyone grows.

Peers

Just as a child needs to work through developmental tasks to achieve trust, autonomy, purpose, and initiative, the adult needs to be aware of predictable adult crises and to be willing to move through them. Peers are an invaluable resource for supporting the teacher's personal and professional growth. Their similar frame of reference furnishes an environment of support. They offer empathy and practical advice. Peers support one another's growth.

Team teaching can be a challenge. Too often. it is entered into without the necessary basis of understanding. Many team teachers are simply mismatched. A mutual philosophy and similar tolerance levels are characteristics of an effective team. The following example illustrates how two teachers are willing to build their relationship on a foundation of communication and understanding. Their work together will be supportive of each other and their children.

Charlene and Marie were hired to team teach in a preschool. They have both taught before. When they meet at the preservice teachers' meeting, they decide to spend time discussing each person's philosophy and classroom practices to insure their effectiveness as a team.

After discussing their expectations for the children, the physical environment, the curriculum, and the role of the teacher, they discuss their own limits. They realize how important it is for teachers to understand their own limits in order to provide children with clear guidelines. They utilize the chart in "The Child's World," Assessment of Teacher Tolerance Levels (fig. 15; see also fig. 13).

	High	Medium	Low
Noise		M	C
Activity	M		C
Mess			M C
Oppositional Behavior	M C		
Disagreement	M C		

M = Marie
C = Charlene

Fig. 15. Assessment of Teacher Tolerance Levels

Noise

Charlene and Marie look at the first item, *noise,* and ask, "What do we mean by noise?" Marie defines noise as a productive hum. "I can tolerate productive humming; but when the noise becomes unproductive, my tolerance goes down, and I have to take action." Marie marks her tolerance as *medium* by putting an M (for Marie) in the appropriate box. Charlene has to admit that she has problems accepting noise. Even a high level of productive noise bothers her. She says, "I know I should be more tolerant of noise, but I'm not. It is an area where I need to grow." She puts a C (for Charlene) in the box for low tolerance.

Activity

To Marie, *activity* means involvement. She loves to see concurrent activities. She defines *learning* as sustained interest in an activity over a period of time. She decides to put her M in the high tolerance area. A lot of activities going on simultaneously bother Charlene. She puts her C in the space for low tolerance under activity.

Mess

Mess is defined as leaving the equipment and supplies out until clean-up time. Both Charlene and Marie agree that they have a low tolerance for mess. They expect the children to put equipment and supplies away when they finish with them. If a child wants to leave a block construction out, it can remain, but in an orderly fashion. They both mark low.

Oppositional Behavior
Charlene and Marie understand the young child's need to engage in oppositional behavior. They have strong backgrounds in child development and feel that a teacher needs to help children develop positive self-concepts and self-discipline. They both put their marks in the high tolerance box under *oppositional behavior.*

Disagreement
Disagreement refers to the children's verbal arguments. Charlene and Marie decide that they both have a high tolerance for disagreement supported by the proper environment. Disagreement leads to creative problem solving. They both mark a high tolerance for disagreement.

Parents
Parents provide teachers with additional adult perspective. They are able to inform the teacher about the child's history and home life. The teacher understands children in general, but the parent understands the individual child better than anyone else. Together they can be an effective team. Parents and teachers provide opportunities for growth, enriching one another as well as the child.

Ramona, who is twenty, works as a teacher at the Early Time Day-Care Center. She is there when the parents drop their children off in the morning. Initially, the parents greet her with a "good morning" and other amenities. But, as the year progresses, the parents have begun to perceive Ramona as a friend and confidant. They tell her many of their problems. Often, they ask her for advice. Ramona begins to feel overloaded by their problems. She doesn't know what to say and feels burdened by the emotional involvement. Ramona does not consider these parents to be her friends, but they appear to view her as a friend.

Ramona discusses this problem with her director, Lola Helms. Lola has attended a conference where this topic was discussed. The seminar leader indicated that working parents are hurried parents. They have little time for intimate relationships. Therefore, teachers, whom they see on a daily basis, begin to be viewed as friends. Lola tells Ramona to use the three communication responses described in chapter 10, "Creative Problem Solving." She assures Ramona, "Your only responsibility is to listen. If the problems are serious,

108

CARIN PANKROS, AGE 5.

send them to me, and I will recommend community resources, such as counseling."

It is reassuring to Ramona to know that other teachers are having similar experiences and that she is not responsible for providing the parents with answers. She looks forward to using the communication responses with adults. Ramona finds it rewarding to work with a director who provides specific guidelines and supports her ability to communicate with parents. She approaches parents with a new sense of self-assurance. Ramona gains confidence and purpose as she practices the communication responses.

Lola also feels a sense of satisfaction from this experience. One of her teachers has come to her with a problem. She was able to provide current professional information and to guide Ramona into an extended understanding of the communication responses. She views her successful handling of the situation as evidence that she is moving toward a positive resolution of the generativity/ stagnation crisis.

Parents often turn to teachers for help in resolving problems with their children. When teachers utilize the communication responses and their understanding of development, they are often able to provide meaningful support. Just as both Lola and Ramona were benefited by their conversation, parent/teacher interactions can be mutually supportive and can benefit the child as well.

Linda Bouti, a mother of a six-year-old, a four-year-old, and a newborn, walks hesitantly into Mrs. Frances's room. After pouring Mrs. Bouti a cup of coffee, Mrs. Frances asks her about the new baby. Mrs. Bouti bursts into tears. She proceeds to tell Mrs. Frances about the physical complications the infant is experiencing.

"But," she says, "That's not why I'm here. I'm concerned about Sean, my four-year-old. He is a different child since the arrival of the baby. He used to be so happy and independent—really a joy. Since the arrival of the baby, he is a changed child. He hangs on me, cries most of the time, and is actually *mean*. I can't believe some of the things he does. I know I'm not supposed to, but I spank him. I even tell him to stop crying and be a good boy. I don't know what has happened to him. Can you tell me what to do?"

Again, Mrs. Frances utilizes the creative problem-solving procedures identified in chapter 10. In addition to listening and respecting Mrs. Bouti's ideas and feelings, she explains how siblings feel when a new baby arrives. She suggests that Sean needs assurance that mother still loves him. "He needs your presence, patience, and attention." Mrs. Frances suggests that she take Sean with her when she runs errands, such as to the grocery store, that she sit next to him when she watches television, and, most importantly, that she spend time alone with him—even ten minutes a day.

Mrs. Bouti says, "You mean that I shouldn't spank him?" Mrs. Frances continues, "Right now he needs to know that you love him. Take time and use the methods that we use in our preschool." Mrs. Bouti has volunteered to assist in the preschool and is aware of the modeling, supporting, and correcting techniques demonstrated in Mrs. Frances's class. Mrs. Bouti muses, "This might sound strange, but I never thought about using these techniques at home."

Periodically, Mrs. Bouti calls Mrs. Frances to discuss Sean's progress and to enlist adult support in handling the crisis that she and her family are experiencing with a seriously ill infant. Six months later Mrs. Frances receives a note from Mrs. Bouti. It says:

Thank you for knowing about child development, for supporting me, and for helping me to understand Sean. All three boys are doing well, and I am grateful to have children who again love and care for each other.

Conclusion

The development of self-discipline is the work of a lifetime. Teachers of young children stand in awe of the enormous growth in social understanding that occurs during the first six years of life.

They have an equal respect for the increasingly complex task of negotiating the stages of adult development. The environment of discipline is created by teachers who understand the scope of human growth. The teacher models, supports, and corrects the child in his attempt to become self-disciplined. She nurtures her own ability to be an authentic and effective teacher by supporting her developing self-discipline. She works at developing an accurate and accepting view of herself and others. She enjoys learning and assumes control over her life. Her personal philosophy enables her to speak and to act from conviction. The environment of discipline promotes the growth of all who enter its circle of support.

Nine

Creativity

Norman Cousins (1979) describes the change he observed in Pablo Casals as the stooped, arthritic old man shuffled to his piano, raised his swollen, clenched fingers, and began to play his beloved Bach.

I was not prepared for the miracle that was about to happen. The fingers slowly unlocked and reached toward the keys like the buds of a plant toward the sunlight. His back straightened. He seemed to breathe more freely. Now his fingers settled on the keys. Then came the opening bars of Bach's Wohltemperierte Klavier, *played with sensitivity and control. . . . Then he plunged into a Brahms concerto and his fingers, now agile and powerful, raced across the keyboard with dazzling speed. His entire body seemed fused with the music; it was no longer stiff and shrunken but supple and graceful and completely freed of its arthritic coils.* [pp. 72, 73]

An artist, such as Don Pablo, commits a lifetime to the development of creative ability. He possesses a high degree of inner discipline. The creativity and the discipline are closely entwined. His deep love of music provides him with a continuous, transforming joy in the disciplined exercise of his talent. He understands the structure of music and the limits of the instrument before he achieves the freedom of individual expression.

Many early childhood educators have observed the transformation of a child caught up in the intensity of creative learning. While the change is not so dramatic as the above example, it exhibits the same elements. As the child becomes mentally absorbed, his body relaxes and turns itself entirely to the accomplishment of the task before him. A child who is involved in creative discovery is in control of himself. When a classroom is characterized by creative learning, discipline-related problems are minimized.

This chapter considers the relationship between creativity and discipline. It illustrates how to build creative opportunities into the early childhood environment. It focuses on the following key environmental elements—room arrangement, equipment, supplies, play, and the teacher (fig. 16).

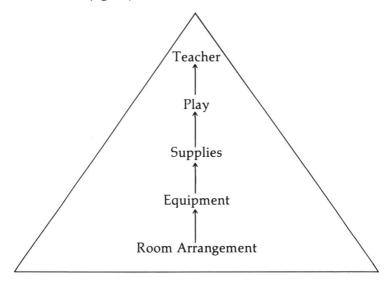

A creative environment is built by starting with room arrangement, adding appropriate equipment and supplies, and providing activities that stimulate play. At the top of these variables stands the teacher, who creates and continues to affect the environment.

Fig. 16. Environmental Variables

The following discussion of creativity in an early childhood environment is based on personal teaching experiences. The example describes one possible expression of the principles of creative learning. A creative classroom reflects both the teacher who sets the stage and the children who play the roles. The classroom described is a group of children between the ages of three and seven. The children were studying England because a member of the class was from England and had much to share with her friends.

Building Creative Opportunities into the Early Childhood Environment
As the visitor enters the room, he is struck by the sense of life and activity. Much is occurring simultaneously, and there is a loud

hum of voices and sounds. Yet, there exists a clear sense of control, and the hum is agreeable; no harsh sounds jar the murmur of discovery and comraderie. At a table three children busily collage all sorts of materials—plastic, styrofoam, cloth, paper—onto large sheets of cardboard with glue and banana tape. Four children have built a road of wooden blocks around a castlelike structure (paper cups atop blocks form the turrets). As the children march around the wall, they spontaneously chant, "They're changing guard at Buckingham Palace. Christopher Robin goes down with Alice. They're changing guard . . ." Two boys in oversized shirts paint a carton taller than themselves with wide brushes. "It's going to be Big Ben, you know, the famous clock in London," says Tom without stopping his work. Next to the windows, Mauricio carefully waters cartons of seedlings. "Why are some plants taller than others?" asks the visitor. "Oh, they got more water to drink," he responds confidently. "This one didn't grow. It's Jenny's rock. I guess it didn't get enough water." He hands the visitor a magnifying glass for a closer look. At a small table two children have a set of plastic alphabet letters. "You count the red ones. I'll count the blue—one, two, . . ." Up on a loft two girls with magic markers and a stack of paper and books are seriously producing picture after picture after picture. In a corner that is furnished as a miniature kitchen, Michael pours an imaginary cup of coffee for his teacher, who is pretending to munch on a sandwich made of wooden puzzle shapes. Michael joins her for "coffee" and some conversation. Just as Tina's and Bill's racing of the large wooden trucks appears to be getting out of hand, the teacher informs them that it is time for the truckers to take a coffee break. They park the trucks and rush to the kitchen, where Michael takes two more cups out of the cupboard. In a small rocker Susie sits peacefully "reading" *Peter Pan.* Next to her are two children playing with a tub of shells. In a far corner the second teacher helps a group of children tack large sheets of butcher paper to the wall. She then pours glue into cups, explaining to Joy how to dilute it with water. Chris carries scissors to the area and others join him in cutting sheets of wallpaper from sample books. They begin to "paper the wall." As the visitor approaches this area, the teacher stands back to observe. "The children were gluing paper onto the wall," she said. "Since that was not acceptable, I suggested that we needed to prepare the wall before gluing up new wallpaper. They suggested the butcher paper." She turned back to the children, "Oh, you're picking such colorful papers. This area will be much brighter when you are finished."

Room Arrangement

The early childhood environment that is arranged according to the learning-center concept described in chapter 5 is rich in creative

ALYSA STOWE, AGE 8.

opportunities and presents a variety of options. The child is able to choose where he will play. As he plays, he begins to define his problems, such as:

Which puzzle will I work?

How can I make it taller?

What will I use for a train?

These problems grow naturally out of a child's play. Once the problem has been defined, the child has begun to implement the creative process. There are four steps to this process:

1. Problem Formation
2. Data Gathering
3. Resolution
4. Evaluation

A major advantage of the learning-center arrangement is the freedom the child has to define his own problem. Teachers who are familiar with the body of information devoted to the subject of motivation will appreciate the advantage of self-selection of task. When a four-year-old in the example "becomes" a guard at Buckingham Palace, he needs to solve the problem of how to put turrets on the castle, even when there are no blocks that fill this function for him. Thus, the child who found paper cups in the kitchen and added

ELSPETH STOWE, AGE 9.

them to the block area was actively participating in the creative process:

1. Problem Formation: "How can I add turrets to this castle?"
2. Data Gathering: "The picture in the book showed them as round. No shapes here are round. I will walk around the room and try to find something that looks right. Those paper cups would work if I cut a design into them. If it is okay with my teacher, I will try them."
3. Resolution: The child obtains permission and cuts the cups to the desired shape. He sets them atop the structure.
4. Evaluation: The child looks at the castle and determines that the problem has been satisfactorily resolved.

Equipment

A creative environment allows the child to utilize materials in whatever nondestructive way he would like. It is wise to select equipment that is versatile and encourages the child to utilize his imagination. Availability of open-ended equipment, which challenges the child to stretch his creative capacities, is a factor in stimulating the creative process.

A college student was asked to make a piece of early childhood equipment that was durable, instructional, self-correcting, and open-ended. She considered a "lock board"—a piece of wood fitted with a variety of locks for the child to explore and manipulate. This idea satisfied the initial three criteria, but it did not seem to her to be sufficiently open-ended. Finally, the student determined to build five wooden nesting boxes, each fitted with a different type of lock. When the boxes were completed, she placed them in the dramatic play center of an early childhood facility. The children noticed a locked box. They opened it and were delighted to find another. Each lock presented a new problem which, when resolved, unlocked the way to the next delightful problem. The locks themselves remained a challenge for some time. However, when the children began to tire of manipulating the locks, they discovered fresh uses for the boxes. They used them as suitcases and packed them for fantasy trips. They lined them up as steps and practiced walking up and down. They built towers and discovered principles of balance. The college student was richly rewarded for her construction work and was happy that she had stretched her own imagination to come up with an open-ended product.

Not all equipment in the early childhood environment can be classified as open-ended. Much equipment suggests a specific use. A teacher may extend the creative potential of this type of equipment by encouraging children to discover unusual uses. Shape puzzles are used by placing the shape into its appropriate space. This is a valid learning experience. As a child manipulates the puzzle, he develops classification systems, terminology, awareness of positive and negative space, visual discrimination, and fine motor control. But what if he decides, like the child in the example, to take the puzzle pieces out of the manipulative area and use them as parts of a sandwich in the dramatic play center? A teacher may view this action as:

- unsystematic ("puzzles belong *here*").
- destructive ("the pieces will be lost").
- disruptive ("if I let this happen, the children will carry equipment all over the room and I will lose control").

This situation demonstrates the importance of systematically thinking through a philosophy of discipline (see chapter 4). This philosophy will be the foundation for a decision regarding the puzzle pieces. Once the teacher has established an environment that has clearly established limits, is secure and trusting, is structured according to the developmental needs of her children, and is rich in activities and opportunities, she may feel comfortable allowing the child to use the puzzle pieces in imaginative dramatic play—as illustrated in the example—or she may decide that removal of the puzzle parts will make her feel uncomfortable. In this case, she will help

the child find an alternative, such as cutting shapes out of construction paper to use as food. She is able to ground her decision on a
carefully considered philosophical basis. She understands her own
feelings and priorities. She communicates her approval of the
child's idea, and she accepts or limits the behavior in a nonjudgmental and supportive manner. She realizes that removal of the
puzzle pieces is not:

- unsystematic (it conforms to the child's own classification system—green equals lettuce, red equals tomato, brown equals
  hamburger).
- destructive (it has been clearly established that when a child is
  finished with a piece of equipment, he returns it to its proper
  space).
- disruptive (the child understands the appropriateness of the
  behavior—it is a reasonable response to a legitimate need and
  is an example of the creative process at work).

Supplies

Many early childhood facilities find it necessary to provide quality care on a minimal amount of capital. This situation, while re-
grettable, can have the effect of stimulating the creative potential of
the adult caregivers. Early childhood personnel often become
skilled at the art of collecting society's cast-offs and making them
the stimulus for learning.

When the development of creativity is a major goal of an early
childhood program, these free materials play an additional role to
the financial considerations. An investment in expensive supplies is
often accompanied by a psychological investment in their use. ("I
spent a lot of money on this paper. This picture had better be
good.") A teacher feels free to allow her children a wider latitude
for experimentation when supplies are free.

In the given example, two girls are seated in a loft with magic
markers, books, and paper. Throughout the course of the morning
these girls look through the books, converse, and draw pictures.
Their teacher feels comfortable about the amount of paper they
consume because it is odd-sized ends that would have been thrown
out by a printer. As the girls continued this activity over a period of
weeks, they began to teach themselves to read.

Imagine a different scene, one where all paper was purchased
from a supply house. Imagine the same two girls beginning to
"scribble" on sheet after sheet of construction paper. Almost any
teacher would feel obliged to limit their activities. Few facilities
could afford to support such expensive work, particularly over an

extended period of time. As a result, a prime learning experience would have been cut off rather than nurtured.

A second demonstration of this principle occurs in the classroom example at the collage table. A variety of collage materials had been introduced over several months. Small amounts of these materials were available to the children on the art cart, but interest in them had waned. The teacher had considered removing the materials and replacing them with something fresh. At the grocery store she noticed bright yellow banana tape and asked for a roll. The next morning she set out large pieces of cardboard and the new tape. This was enough to inspire a renaissance of collage work. A particularly rewarding aspect of this experience occurred when a five-year-old boy, who had recently become unruly and lacking in direction, became excited about this project. He worked on it for two full hours, using his whole body to glue and tape several layers of objects onto the backdrop. He chanted and sang as he worked, "I'm making a yucky picture, a yucky, yucky picture. This is my yucky picture." The finished product, known affectionately as "Brett's Yucky Picture," hung on the wall for the rest of the school year. Many visitors to the school commented that it looked like something one would see in a museum of contemporary art. Brett felt proud of his work and himself.

A child was benefited by a teacher's ability to be aware of appropriate classroom materials in her adult world, and a discipline problem was relieved as the child expressed himself creatively.

Play

As the visitor viewed the early childhood environment described in the example, he was aware of children who were busy, in control of themselves, and intensely involved in their work. It was exciting, but puzzling. His personal schema of school involved desks, books, and a teacher at the blackboard. This unfamiliar learning environment prompted him to wonder exactly how and what the children were learning.

Children learn as they play. What they learn ranges from an acceptance of self and others to a feeling of competence to such specific skills as cutting on a line with scissors or zipping a zipper. Play is a valuable vehicle for learning because it allows the player to formulate his own problem (step one of the creative process). It opens doors to potentially unlimited learning.

Brian Sutton-Smith (1975) has spoken of play as novelty training (open-ended responses). He has stated that "there is no creativity that doesn't come from play." A problem that develops in a play situation rarely has one right solution. As children play, they gain

CATHERINE PANKROS, AGE 3.

experience in formulating a variety of novel responses. Through their play they develop flexibility, diversity, novelty, and competence. A play situation allows a child to take risks, even to risk failure and, having failed, to add what he has learned to his data bank and to try again.

Children who play become adults who are capable of open-ended thinking. For example, the aborigines live in a dry, sparse environment. They need to be flexible, novel, and solution-oriented in order to survive. They encourage their children to play. They seem to know intuitively that children who play will learn to be more inventive and resourceful (Sutton-Smith 1975).

What has been traditionally true for the aborigine people is even more true for western civilization today. In the face of problems of enormous complexity, need exists to cultivate future citizens who are capable of insightful, disciplined thinking that is original and inventive. Jean Piaget expands upon this idea:

The principal goal of education is to create men who are capable of doing new things, not simply of repeating what other generations have done—men who are creative, inventive and discoverers. The second goal of education is to form minds which can be critical, can verify, and not accept everything they are offered. The great danger today is of slogans, collective opinions, ready-made trends of thought. We have to be able to resist individually, to criticize, to distinguish between what is proven and what is not. So we need pupils who are active, who learn early to find out by themselves, partly by their own spontaneous activity and partly through materials we set up for them; we learn early to tell what is verifiable and what is simply the first idea to come to them [Elkind 1970, p. 25].

In looking at the children in the example, we have seen something of the intensity of play. One child, having seen pictures of a castle with turrets, would not give up until he had reproduced a reasonable facsimile. Two girls became so engrossed in drawing and copying out of books that they eventually taught themselves to read. A disruptive child became so involved in his collage work that he was productive for an entire morning and consistently more productive as he basked in the good feelings of accomplishment and recognition.

Piaget has identified three stages of play—sensorimotor play, symbolic play, and games with rules. The initial stage, sensorimotor play, involves basic sensorial manipulation of materials and is frequently observed in the preschool-aged child. The two children in the example who are playing with shells are able to use their senses in the construction of knowledge. As they observe, feel, sort, and manipulate the shells, they are building a familiarity with natural phenomena that leads to further learning.

Piaget's second stage of play is symbolic play (one object represents another, as when puzzle pieces become parts of a sandwich). The highest expression of symbolic play is dramatic play. The primary accomplishment of Piaget's preoperational child is the mastery of the symbolic function. When a child is involved in dramatic play, he translates his observations of life into a symbolic form. As he dramatizes a role, he is the symbolizer as well as the symbol. He uses his body as a symbol, just as the adult employs the written word. When Michael served coffee in the classroom example, he recalled his parents working in the kitchen; he classified and organized his observations; he expressed his information symbolically through the medium of dramatic play. This example illustrates the fact that play is more than imitation. As a child plays he organizes, synthesizes, and interprets his experiences. Play is a symbolic abstraction, and as such it becomes the highest and most appropriate form of math and reading readiness.

A final reference to the classroom example clarifies the role of dramatic play as a means of organizing information. The children in this classroom had been learning about England. They viewed a slide show of the changing of the guard at Buckingham Palace and saw other sights such as Big Ben. They listened to the stories "Madeline in London," "The Guard Mouse," "Winnie the Pooh," and "Peter Pan." They heard the poems of A. A. Milne. At this point the children had been exposed to much new information. They needed opportunities to integrate the new concepts into their present mental constructs. This was accomplished through dramatic play. One group of children invented and constructed an elaborate block version of Buckingham Palace. They then "became" the palace guards marching around the structure chanting A. A. Milne's familiar lines. Others carefully painted the tall packing box that their teacher had placed in the room. These boys "were" the engineers who designed and created the world-famous clock. Finally, in a small rocker in the center of a busy, noisy classroom, sat Susie, who was no longer Susie, but was Wendy flying across the London rooftops to share in the adventures of Peter and the lost boys.

Here is a picture of totally integrated learning. The children have recalled and systematized their information and then translated it into a symbolic form. The imagination utilized in play anticipates the representation of reading and writing (Sutton-Smith 1975).

Piaget's highest level of play is the playing of games with rules. This ability to play games with rules involves a loss of egocentrism which does not occur until around age eight. The young child begins to function within a set of prestated rules when he plays such games as Duck-Duck-Goose or Tag. When games are introduced into the early childhood environment, it is important for the teacher to modify the rules to fit the developmental level of the child.

The Teacher

When a room full of children demonstrates creativity that integrates inner discipline, a teacher has set the stage. The role of the teacher is the single most important element in the nurturing of creative learning. She prepares the physical environment by arranging learning centers for optimal use, by equipping centers with open-ended equipment and supplies, and by utilizing free and inexpensive materials. She plans a curriculum that stimulates curiosity and imagination. She exposes children to new ideas and experiences through literature, poetry, media, field trips, community resources, discussion, music, and "whatever." She provides rich opportunities for the construction and internalization of knowledge through play.

In addition to creating an appropriate physical environment and curriculum, the teacher carefully structures the psychological climate. The psychological climate is comfortable and trusting when limits are clearly set. A person is free to be creative and to take risks when he knows the rules. In this respect, creativity and conformity are not antithetical. The key factor is that the teacher determines how much and what type of conformity she requires. Young children need the freedom to explore their creative potential, and they need rules that encourage the development of self-actualization and empathy. Rules need to be simple, clear, and behavior oriented. In fact, it is possible to conduct a classroom with only one rule—you may not hurt yourself or anyone else. When this rule is interpreted physically and psychologically, it covers every unacceptable behavior, including care of materials (see chapter 7, "The Child's World").

Just as a rigid, authoritarian atmosphere in the early childhood classroom stifles individual expression, a permissive or "anything goes" atmosphere creates confusion (see fig. 17). A creative atmosphere provides limits that support and guide. This atmosphere encourages the development of empathy and cooperation among the group, allows for the growth of discipline within the individual, and leads to the resolution of problems between people.

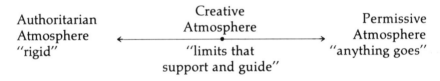

Fig. 17. The Creative Atmosphere

The primary influence on the psychological atmosphere of the classroom is the teacher herself. She establishes a disciplined and trusting environment that is alive with creativity by modeling qualities and behaviors for her children to emulate. When a teacher feels comfortable with herself, she is able to work toward an enjoyment of life, an ability to make mistakes, an ability to have ideas and be open to the ideas of others, a respect for each child, and an ability to see the relationship between ideas.

Enjoyment of Life

When teachers enjoy life, they communicate this sense of joy to the people around them. Children sense that a playful attitude is not childish but is rather a characteristic of mature self-acceptance.

Ability to Make Mistakes

Teachers who admit what they do not know and point out their own mistakes make an enormous contribution to the mental health

Fig. 18. *Characteristics of the Teacher Who Promotes Creativity*

of their children. When children feel comfortable with their mistakes, they are able to implement the creative process and accept their own humanity.

Ability to Have Ideas and Be Open to the Ideas of Others

When a teacher is excited about life and exhibits an interest in the world around her, she influences the children's attitudes toward learning. When she brings ideas to the classroom and accepts the ideas of the children, learning becomes a shared adventure.

Respect for Each Child

Most teachers accept the value of "respecting" the child. However, it is only as the teacher begins to feel a genuine respect for herself that she is able to respect others. This becomes the first link of a chain. As the teacher accepts herself and the child, the child is able to accept himself and others.

Ability to See the Relationship between Ideas

A week after listening to the story of *Frederick*, a poetic field mouse who gathered up the sun's warmth for the cold winter months, a young boy tugged on his teacher's shirt and said, "Teacher, I feel the warmth from the sun's rays, just like Frederick." Teachers need to be as wise as this.

Ten

Creative Problem Solving

"Research results of Getzels and Jackson (1962), Guilford (1967), Mand (1974), Torrance (1972), and Yawkey (1978) show that development of creative thought is significantly related to growth of social relationships" (Yawkey 1980). *Creating Discipline in the Early Childhood Classroom* has demonstrated how an understanding of human development, environment, and curriculum leads to the type of creative learning described in chapter 9. As Yawkey points out, there is a significant relationship between the development of creative thinking and the growth of social relationships. Children who employ the creative process in their play can be taught to utilize effective communication skills and ultimately to solve interpersonal problems.

Chapter 10, "Creative Problem Solving," enumerates the steps that lead children to an ability to solve problems. The process is difficult to understand because skillful teachers appear to implement it naturally. An observer may think that he has simply stumbled onto a group of intelligent and well-brought-up children. In fact, the teacher works consistently at guiding her class in a carefully prepared environment. She builds trust. She models and teaches communication techniques. She eases her children into the process of creative problem solving.

Miss Pat's preschool class consists of a group of three-, four-, and five-year-old children. While the children are active and noisy, the classroom remains calm and purposeful. The children have learned to disagree and to talk out their conflicts because Miss Pat has taught them the process of creative problem solving. Creative problem solving emerges from an ability to communicate.

Communication is a process of interaction between two or more people for the purposes of enjoyment, giving information, or solving problems. Meaningful communication occurs when each person possesses listening abilities and nonverbal and verbal communication skills.

Through the communication process young children, with the help of adults, can learn to solve the problems that arise in the classroom. They learn to talk out their differences. Discussing a problem often takes time. The more practice children have, the more proficient they become. As time goes on, children need less teacher direction and are able to do more on their own.

Miss Pat's children are learning that it is acceptable to disagree. They are also learning how to listen to one another and to discuss problems and difficulties. Though they often need help to solve their dilemmas, they are beginning to talk with and help each other. Through the continued support of Miss Pat, the children are developing a trust in one another, their teacher, and their environment.

Building Trust

As a student of human development, Miss Pat realizes that meaningful human interaction begins with trust. To assure the development of meaningful relationships, Miss Pat demonstrates trusting behaviors in her classroom. She expresses trust through her interest in each child, her willingness to listen, and her nonjudgmental reactions. She is aware of messages sent through nonverbal communication and uses body language to enhance the growth of trust.

Miss Pat conveys interest in the children by her morning greeting. When Erik is brought to school by his dad, Miss Pat says, "Good morning, Erik," and then exchanges a few words with the parent, usually something light and personal, such as, "How was your potluck dinner last night?" As the parent and teacher talk, Erik goes to his cubby, takes off his coat, and begins an activity. Before leaving, Erik's dad waves good-bye and is off for the day.

After all of the children have arrived, Miss Pat walks around to say hello. She talks with each child or small group of children and asks questions. When a child is unable to initiate an activity or is having difficulty settling down, Miss Pat asks him where he would like to work for the day. She then accompanies him to a learning center and helps him get started. Each of these brief, but personal, interactions demonstrates Miss Pat's interest in the child.

Miss Pat continues to build a trusting relationship with each of her children by listening to them. In her morning conversations, Miss Pat listens to more than words. She is sensitive to the feelings being expressed and to the messages being conveyed by the children's bodies. By assimilating words, feelings, and body language, Miss Pat understands what is being communicated by the children. Darlene runs through the front door and waves her arms about as she says, "We have a new kitty. Her name is Buttons, and my mom says we can bring her to school." Miss Pat feels and shares the

ALYSA STOWE, AGE 8.

excitement expressed by Darlene's words and movements, and she bends down to talk with Darlene about the new cat. As she moves toward the door to greet the next child, she turns to Darlene to remind her of the cat puppet in the language center. "You could pretend that it is your new cat and tell her about school to prepare her for her visit."

One of the most difficult aspects of building trust is listening without being judgmental. Nonjudgmental listening absorbs what the other person is saying without formulating conclusions or opinions. Most people listen from their own point of view and draw judgmental conclusions. Miss Pat has developed a sensitivity that allows her to hear what the children tell her without judging it to be right or wrong. She communicates acceptance through her verbal and nonverbal language. She encourages the children to speak openly. Miss Pat spends much of her teaching time interacting with children in the learning centers.

When she taught first grade, it frustrated her not to be able to listen to the children in the morning. They rushed in eager to tell her what had happened on the playground or to report on a favorite television program, but she had to send them to their seats in order to have milk money and attendance records ready on time.

Toward the end of her first week as a preschool teacher, Miss Pat was sitting on the edge of the sandbox with a small group of children. She realized that in this new setting she was able to do what she had never had enough time for in elementary school—talk with the children. Her genuine enjoyment of their conversations is felt by the children, who laugh and talk comfortably with their teacher.

Teachers who possess effective communication skills are aware of the messages given through body language or nonverbal behavior. They continue to build a trusting relationship through appropriate nonverbal language skills. The dimensions of body language include the following:

- *Personal space*—the distance between people.
- *Eye contact*—visual field directed at the other person.
- *Face and head movements*—the conscious and unconscious movements of the head and parts of the face.
- *Hand and arm movements*—the conscious and unconscious movements of the hands, fingers, and arms.
- *Total body movement*—the conscious and unconscious movements of the body.
- *Physical contact*—the act of touching another person.

Each person has an inherent personal space or "comfort zone." For most people this is approximately two or three feet. Violations of personal space are seen in the early childhood classroom, as when Meredith is playing by herself. Her face tenses as Amy brushes against her. "Go away!" shouts Meredith at the invader, who has already moved on. Teachers often stop children's disagreements by simply moving them apart, placing an object between them, or moving several children out of a crowded area.

When Miss Pat talks with a child, she stoops down to his level, remembering to begin the conversation about two feet away. As the conversation progresses, she moves closer. By not intruding into the child's personal space, Miss Pat puts the child at ease.

Eye contact tells the child that he has his teacher's attention. Receiving the teacher's full attention makes the child feel important, and he continues the conversation with confidence.

Face and head movements encourage further communication. A slight, periodic nodding of the head demonstrates interest and a desire to hear more. A nod expresses acceptance of what is being said. It says, "I understand."

Hand and arm movements communicate the same message: "Please continue." Miss Pat can be seen gently extending an arm toward a child as she converses. This type of simple, spontaneous gesture toward the child demonstrates appreciation of him and his words.

JENNIFER ZAMARIN, AGE 4.

When a teacher's total body is relaxed and attentive, children sense sincerity. Miss Pat bends down to talk with a child at his level. This is one of the best ways for a teacher to show that she really wants to communicate. Her whole body says, "You are important to me." This body posture gives the child a real sense of security and makes him feel special.

Physical contact evidences a high trust level between people. A teacher demonstrates trust by touching a child. The child exhibits trust in his teacher by touching her and by allowing her to touch him. Touching another person communicates warmth, confidence, and caring. Miss Pat often places her hand on a child's shoulder or knee. She shakes hands, hugs, and holds a child in her lap.

Physical contact is a very effective nonverbal behavior. It usually enables even the most quiet child to relax and open up. However, either an extremely passive or an extremely aggressive child may be mistrustful of touching. A sensitive teacher respects these feelings and continues to work at building trust until touching results.

Communication Responses

Early childhood educators build a trustful relationship with each child in the group by expressing genuine interest, listening to what the child has to say, responding nonjudgmentally, and employing appropriate body language. At the same time, the teacher utilizes verbal responses that encourage the child to continue talking. Skillful responses also help the child understand what he is saying and feeling. They clarify his thoughts.

Three verbal responses support optimal communication and problem solving in the early childhood classroom. These communication responses are the *continuing response,* the *content response,* and the *feeling response.* The teacher uses these responses as she talks with the children. Sometimes one response is adequate; at other times, a combination of responses is made use of. Each time a teacher employs a communication response, she models effective communication for the children. Eventually young children use these responses as they talk to each other.

The Continuing Response

The *continuing response* encourages the child to talk and to feel comfortable with his thoughts. The teacher's role is to help the child feel good about conveying his thoughts and to share in the joy of communication. She does this by periodically saying, "Ah," "Uh huh," "Yes," "I see," or similar sounds and words. At the same time the teacher employs the body language described earlier in this chapter, such as nodding her head, reaching toward the child, or touching his arm. The mechanics of the continuing response are simple; however, knowing when to use this technique takes time and practice.

Example 1

> Melinda: My ballerina costume is torn.
> Miss Pat: Oh.
> Melinda: I put it on last night and ripped it on the doorknob.
> Miss Pat: Uh huh. (She nods her head.)
> Melinda: Mommy is going to sew it. I love my ballerina costume.
> (Melinda runs off to play.)

The Content Response

The *content response* is the second communication response, which encourages the child to continue talking and to work through simple problems. The teacher "mirrors" back or repeats what the child has said. When Tom says, "I can't find my comb," Miss Pat says, "You can't find your comb." This mirroring back has several effects. First, it tells the child that his teacher is listening. Second, it assures the teacher that she has accurately heard what was said because the child is able to correct her content response. Third, it assures the child that he has been understood. If the teacher's content response does not reflect what the child intended to say, he has the opportunity to rephrase.

The importance of this skill cannot be overemphasized. Miss Pat uses the content response throughout the day.

Example 2

Manuel comes running into the room.
Manuel: I have a new baby.
Miss Pat: Manuel, you have a new baby!
Manuel: Yes, his name is Romero.
Miss Pat: Oh, your new baby's name is Romero.
Manuel: He is not at home.
Miss Pat: Romero is not at home?
Manuel: No, he is in the hospital. So is my mother.

Children need help as they manipulate their environment. The content response provides the child with support and time to think through a difficulty. It enables him to develop his thinking skills and seek solutions for himself.

Example 3

Sarah is working with colored pegs and a pegboard. Suddenly, she dumps the box of pegs onto the table.
Sarah: No more red pegs. I need red pegs.
Miss Pat: Sarah, you have run out of red pegs.
Sarah: I want red pegs.
Miss Pat: You need red pegs to work on your design.
Sarah: Yes. (She looks through the pegs on the table.) Oh, look! Here's one!

Children often argue over materials and supplies that are available to everyone. Once again, Miss Pat uses the content response to help the children solve their own difficulty. The content response also helps Miss Pat to ascertain the facts.

132

Example 4

> John and Billy are playing with the dough. They are using
> holiday cookie cutters and a small rolling pin. Both boys
> reach for the rolling pin at the same time. Billy picks it up,
> and John yells at him to share it.
> Miss Pat: I hear an argument at the dough table.
> John: Billy won't share the rolling pin.
> Billy: I got it first.
> Miss Pat: John, you want the rolling pin, but Billy got it first.
> John: Yes, and he won't share.
> Miss Pat: Billy, John thinks you won't share the rolling pin.
> Billy: I will too share. I just want to use it first.
> Miss Pat: John, Billy will share it with you as soon as he is
> finished.

Miss Pat's final response provides indirect guidance. She remains on the scene to be sure that the children act on their decision.

The Feeling Response
The third communication response is the *feeling response.* This response addresses itself to the child's feelings. Just as the content response mirrors back what the child has said, the feeling response mirrors the child's feelings. It demonstrates acceptance of feelings. When a teacher says, "I see that you are upset," she tells the child that being upset is all right. She not only reassures the child that at this school all feelings are accepted, but she also teaches the child about his feelings by labeling them. A child may not realize that his uncomfortable feeling is called anger. Knowing that his feelings are understood and accepted encourages a child to continue to talk.

Often the realization that his teacher understands how he feels is all a child needs. Jill runs up to Miss Pat saying, "Angie took my truck." Miss Pat responds, "That makes you angry." With a satisfied, almost enlightened, look on her face, Jill says, "Yes!" and walks off.

The feeling response clarifies feelings, as the content response clarifies words. When a feeling has been labeled inaccurately, the child is able to correct the teacher's response. When Miss Pat says to Shawna, "You sound unhappy about that," Shawna responds, "No, I don't mind."

Miss Pat extends the feeling response by labeling her own feelings. She provides a model for the children to imitate. She can be heard making the following statements:

- "I feel proud when I see you working so hard on your painting, John."
- "Angie, I feel angry when you throw blocks. Someone could be hurt."
- "I am excited that Darlene's new cat is coming to school tomorrow."

The three communication responses may be used interchangeably. The teacher decides which one to use in a given situation. In three earlier incidents, involving a new baby, red pegs, and a rolling pin, Miss Pat employed the content response. The following examples examine what might have occurred if she had chosen to use the feeling response.

Example 5

Manuel comes running into the room.
Manuel: I have a new baby.
Miss Pat: Manuel, you sound excited.
Manuel: His name is Romero. I love him.
Miss Pat: You feel happy about that.
Manuel: Pretty soon he comes home.
Miss Pat: You are anxious for him to be at home.

Example 6

Sarah is working with the colored pegs and a pegboard. Suddenly, she dumps the box of pegs onto the table.
Sarah:　No more red pegs. I need red pegs.
Miss Pat: You sound frustrated, Sarah.
Sarah:　I am mad. I do not have any more red pegs.
Miss Pat: You are upset that you cannot find red pegs.
Sarah:　Yes. . . . Oh, look. Here's one.

Example 7

John and Billy are playing with the dough. They are using holiday cookie cutters and a small rolling pin. Both boys reach for the rolling pin at the same time. Billy picks it up, and John yells at him to share it.
Miss Pat: I hear an argument at the dough table.
John:　Billy won't share the rolling pin.

Miss Pat: That makes you mad, John.

Billy: But I got it first.

Miss Pat: John is mad, because he thinks you won't share.

Billy: I will too share. I just want to use it first.

Miss Pat: John, Billy will share it with you as soon as he is finished [content response].

John: Okay.

Miss Pat: I'm proud of the way you talk to each other. You solved this problem yourselves. That should make you both happy. (Miss Pat shakes hands with each of the boys.)

John and
Billy: Yes!

The teacher who strives to provide an optimal environment for the children engages in frequent evaluation. Just as she evaluates the room arrangement and educational objectives of a teaching unit, she evaluates her own teaching performance. She knows that a warm, supportive teacher's voice exerts a positive influence on the classroom atmosphere. It increases the effectiveness of the communication responses. An awareness of one's own voice is developed by asking these questions:

- Does my voice have a calm and pleasant tone?
- Does my voice convey confidence?
- Do I use a natural rhythm pattern?
- Do I speak to children as I speak to adults?
- Does my voice vary to fit the occasion?
- Do I avoid overuse of expressions such as "you know" and "okay"?
- Am I aware of the effect my voice has on the classroom atmosphere?

When Miss Pat engages in this sort of self-evaluation, she likes to run the tape recorder during a group time period with her class. After school she listens to the tape in order to analyze her voice.

The communication responses not only clarify ideas, demonstrate understanding and acceptance, and encourage the child to talk and seek solutions, but they also continue the trust-building process. The communication responses are not judgmental. Children who feel accepted and valued are able to relax, experiment, feel good about themselves, and develop competence. They become self-directed. A trusting environment supports the growth of self-discipline.

GREGORY WILMES, AGE 7.

Creative Problem Solving

A primary goal of the early childhood educator is to provide a creative atmosphere which is neither authoritarian nor permissive. This atmosphere provides clear limits and support which encourage inner directedness in the child. When problems arise, the ultimate goal is for children to decide upon their own solutions.

This chapter has demonstrated the problem-solving potential of the communication responses. Often when a young child seeks help or is involved in an uncomfortable situation, he simply needs to know that his teacher understands. At other times, the teacher's calm mirroring of a situation provides the child with the support he needs to find his own solution. There are also times when a child needs a teacher's help in clarifying his difficulty, thinking of possible solutions, choosing a solution, and acting on his decision. This process of creative problem solving mirrors the creative process described in chapter 9.

The Creative Process   Creative Problem Solving

1. Problem formation   1. Problem clarification
2. Data gathering   2. Solution formation

3. Resolution	3. Solution selection
4. Evaluation	4. Implementation

Problem Clarification

The communication responses—the continuing response, the content response, and the feeling response—aid both teacher and children in understanding the problem. Through the communication responses, the facts and feelings of the difficulty emerge. When everyone involved in the incident understands the situation, solutions can be discussed. Taking time for each person to state his perceptions and feelings encourages solutions that are appropriate to all points of view. When this time to promote understanding is rushed, a satisfactory solution is less likely to surface.

Solution Formation

Once teacher and children have discussed and understood the problem, it is possible to discover solutions. Potential solutions are generated through a brainstorming session. Children are encouraged to suggest as many solutions as possible. The teacher may offer suggestions, but not to the exclusion of the children. All suggested solutions are accepted. Often the teacher writes each suggestion on a piece of paper or a blackboard.

Solution Selection

When participants in the creative problem-solving process agree that enough solutions have been generated, the selection process begins. Each suggestion is discussed. The discussion continues until agreement is reached.

Implementation

Before the solution is acted upon, the children are asked to practice with their teacher. A young child may agree to a resolution without understanding how to implement it. The teacher dramatizes the solution with the children. She may take a role or simply direct a scene. Once the teacher determines that the children are ready to put their solution to the test, she encourages them and steps back to observe. When she is satisfied that the children have successfully resolved the problem, she moves away. A sensitive teacher reinforces this successful experience by later reminding the children of their accomplishment, complimenting them, and rejoicing with them.

Example 8

Two children are playing in the dramatic play center, which is set up as a kitchen. Suddenly, David says in an angry voice, "I will not be the baby." Amy responds, "Yes, you will. You are short, and I need a baby." As soon as Miss Pat hears the angry voice, she moves to the dramatic play center, and the problem solving begins.

Problem Clarification

Miss Pat: Sounds like there is a problem over here.

David: I will not be a baby, and she says I have to be.

Amy: I need a baby, and he is short.

Miss Pat: Amy, you want to have a baby to play with. You want David to be the baby, but David does not want to be the baby [content response].

David: I am not a baby.

Miss Pat: You are not a baby, David [content response].

Amy: He can pretend to be a baby.

Miss Pat: You would like David to pretend to be the baby [content response].

David: I will not pretend to be a baby. I am four years old!

Miss Pat: You are angry that Amy wants you to be the baby [feeling response].

David: Yes! I want to be the big brother.

Miss Pat: I see [continuing response].

Amy: But who will be the baby? I can't be the baby. I am the mommy.

Miss Pat: So, Amy wants to be the mommy, and she needs a baby. David wants to be the big brother; he does not want to be the baby [content response].

(Amy and David nod their heads.)

Solution Formation

Miss Pat: Well, how can we solve this problem? Let's think.

David: That doll could be the baby (he points to a doll in a high chair).

Amy: I'll get Brian. He likes to be the baby.

Miss Pat: I could be the baby.

Amy: You're too big!

Miss Pat: Remember, we're thinking of solutions. We'll talk about them later. Do you have any other suggestions?

Amy and
David: No.

Solution Selection

Miss Pat: Okay, you two, let's pick a solution. The first idea was David's. He suggested that you use a doll.

Amy: But I want a real baby.

David: I want a real brother.
Miss Pat: You don't like that idea.
(Amy and David shake their heads.)
Miss Pat: The second idea was Amy's. She wants to ask
           Brian to be the baby.
Amy: Yes, I want Brian to be the baby.
(David nods his head.)
Miss Pat: Now the third idea. I said I would be the baby.
Amy: But you're too big.
David: I want a brother, and you're a girl.
Miss Pat: Then it sounds like you both like the second idea
           best. You want to ask Brian to play with you and
           be the baby?
(Amy and David grin and nod.)
Implementation
Miss Pat: We have decided on a solution. Who is going to
           ask Brian?
Amy and
David: I will.
Miss Pat: Okay. You both want to. What will you say to
           him?
Amy: Will you play house with me? I need a baby.
David: I want you to be my brother.
Miss Pat: Okay. Pretend I am Brian. What will you say to
           me, David?
David: Please come and play with us. I want a brother.
Amy: I want a baby. Please be my baby.
Miss Pat: (Pretending to be Brian) I'll play with you. Come
           on. Okay, you two, go talk with Brian. (The chil-
           dren ask Brian to play with them and he agrees.)
Later that morning as the class is playing outside, Miss Pat
calls Amy and David over. She says, "Do you remember
that earlier today you were very angry with each other?
Amy wanted you to be the baby, David, but you didn't want
to be." The children laugh and nod. "You did a beautiful
job of solving your problem. I am really proud of you. Let's
remember to tell your mothers all about it when they pick
you up today."

Conclusion

The strategies described in this chapter have been widely practiced and found to be successful. A more authoritarian teacher than
Miss Pat may seem to resolve problems quickly, but the effect is

different. Children who respond to an authoritarian adult learn to rely on others to solve their problems. Miss Pat's approach teaches the children to think for themselves. They feel good about themselves, understand their feelings, and respect the feelings of others. They learn to communicate and solve problems. They are becoming self-directed and, ultimately, self-disciplined.

Teachers who practice creative problem solving need to be patient with themselves, building competencies slowly. It is best to focus on one skill at a time. When Miss Pat began to refine her teaching skills, she spent the first month of school concentrating on building trust. The next month she focused on her body language, working to improve it. Throughout the year, she assigned herself a specific skill. She worked on each of the communication responses and concentrated on creative problem solving. It has taken her years of teaching to feel proficient and comfortable with her communication skills, but she feels that it was well worth the effort. Certainly, her children would agree.

Eleven

The Environment of Discipline

Although the fully functioning teacher may be a highly intuitive person, she does not operate on intuition alone. She understands the role of the environment of discipline in nurturing the growth of children and adults.

The teacher creates the environment of discipline by carefully planning the room arrangement and the curriculum according to principles of child development. She establishes a philosophy of discipline and acts on her convictions as she models, supports, and corrects within the circle of support. She nurtures the ability of her children to engage in creative play and instructs them in the art of creative problem solving. The environment of discipline allows interpersonal problems to emerge and be confronted. It supports the growth of self-discipline.

Because the teacher understands this complex process, she is able to explain it to her children's parents. She works consistently and systematically to inform and educate parents. She clearly communicates how self-discipline is nurtured in the early childhood classroom.

Chapter 11, "The Environment of Discipline," describes the teacher's role as she works with parents to promote the child's growth in self-discipline. It provides practical suggestions for communicating with parents and shows how teachers articulate the environment of discipline.

The teacher's primary tool for educating parents is the planned parent/teacher conference. Ancillary tools that support the conference are written materials, visual communication, and personal interaction. These ancillary resources each support the parent/teacher relationship and allow a meaningful conference to be conducted within an atmosphere of mutual trust.

Written Communication
There are three major forms of written communication—the school handbook, the parent newsletter, and personal notes.

The School Handbook

The school handbook is the first written material the parent receives. It is a resource of information. It enhances realistic parental expectations by including a typical schedule of daily activities, an explanation of the learning centers, and a statement of the school's philosophy. This information provides the parent with accurate educational expectations and a sense of security in knowing how the child spends his time at school.

Included in the school handbook is a section on how the school nurtures the child's self-discipline. It provides a rationale for expected child behavior. It may, for instance, explain that children do not run in the classroom because it is not safe to run. It goes on to describe the teacher, who supports the child's self-discipline by stating, "We walk in our room so that no one falls or gets hurt. We want you to be safe." This section in the school handbook explains the philosophy of discipline, expectations for the child, parental responsibilities, and appropriate teacher behaviors. It provides parents with concrete illustrations of how the parents and teacher work together to build the child's self-discipline.

The Parent Newsletter

Another form of written communication is the parent newsletter. Through a regular newsletter, parents remain updated on the happenings at the center. Effective newsletters are short, interesting, and accurate. Included in the newsletter are a calendar of upcoming events, general announcements, and specific classroom incidents. If the director notices that the children are overly "antsy," she may use the newsletter to inform the parents. She may say, "Winter is a difficult time for children. They have so much excess physical energy. In school we go outside every day, regardless of the weather, to get physical exercise. We also spend more time with the large muscle equipment. At home, children need to play outdoors and be involved in large muscle activities, such as riding their Big Wheel in the basement."

Personal Notes

Writing short notes is one of the best ways to inform parents about their child's activities. Notes can explain a complex incident, share a humorous episode, or provide specific information. Regularly written notes provide the parent with additional insight into the child's experience.

The personal note is always positive in tone. If the teacher needs to inform a parent about a problem, she schedules a conference. Positive notes provide a mechanism for the parent to engage in meaningful conversation with the child. A mother may say, "Let's see what Miss Eleanor has to say. She says that you enjoy the poems from *Where the Sidewalk Ends* [Silverstein 1974, pp. 58–59]. Your favorite poem is 'Sick.' Tell me about it."

A teacher may communicate the joyful experience of seeing a four-year-old change his behavior. Miss Eleanor writes, "Jimmy asked Betsy if he could use the block arch for his factory. He is learning to ask for things, instead of grabbing. We are proud of Jimmy." This is wonderful news for a parent! She has an opportunity to build immediately upon the gains that her child is making at school. At home she may say, "I am so happy that you are learning to ask for the things you want in school. You can do it at home, too. Ask Jeremy (Jimmy's brother) if he will split a popsicle. Don't take the popsicle. Ask Jeremy if he will share it with you."

Teachers also use personal notes to answer parents' questions. In response to Kimko's mother's concern about lunch, Miss Eleanor writes, "Kimko ate her entire lunch. She had macaroni and cheese, a hot dog, milk, bread and butter, and an apple."

When writing notes, teachers need to use appropriate paper, legible handwriting, and clear sentences. Some teachers like to ask another staff member to read their notes to be sure that they have expressed themselves accurately.

Visual Communication

The cliché that a picture is worth a thousand words is aptly true in the preschool center. In the school handbook parents are made aware of the special parent area appropriately called, "The Parent Center." This area offers parents several services—a small library containing current articles, magazines, and books; a bulletin board displaying information about upcoming events; a note center holding written messages; and a children's area displaying children's work or photographs. This area communicates a visual message to parents. The library offers parents an opportunity to gather information from respected authorities. This material is read on the parent's own time schedule within the comfort of her home.

The teacher refers the parent to the library materials before or after a conference. The parent may say in passing, "John doesn't want to go to bed at night. I've tried everything; what shall I do?" The teacher has seen an article in the magazine *Parents* providing parental guidelines for assisting children at bedtime. She goes to the library in the parents center and secures the article. Discussing a magazine article written by a third party is an optimal method for problem solving. The teacher mirrors the parent's comments and adds information regarding the relationship between written information and the specific child.

The bulletin board is an ideal resource for keeping parents informed. A simple sign, "Tuition is due Friday," reminds parents of their financial responsibility. It eliminates the task of verbally reminding parents. The bulletin board also informs the parent of upcoming workshops, such as, "Enhancing Self-Discipline," to be held at the next parent meeting.

The note center is a reliable depository for parent-teacher messages. When notes are placed in this area regularly, parents automatically look there for personal messages. When parents write notes to teachers, they are assured that the teacher will receive them.

The children's area provides a specific place for the teacher to extend the parent-teacher communication process. Children's work or photographs may be placed in this area with captions. Miss Eleanor takes a photograph of Jimmy asking Betsy for a block arch and displays it with the caption, "Asking is a major step in self-discipline." She reinforces Jimmy's growth and illustrates to other parents and children the importance of language.

The parent center is generally located in a hall or close to the school entrance. The space can be small and has a chair, table, bookshelves, and the bulletin board. It is an appropriate place for parents to relax as they wait for their child to finish an activity. It allows the parent a few quiet moments without feeling that she is in the way.

Personal Interaction

The heart of parent-teacher communication is personal interaction. This direct communication allows the parent and teacher to work together as a team to provide a consistent and sustaining environment. Three aspects of personal interaction are positive daily contacts, telephone calls, and the parent/teacher conference.

Positive Daily Contacts

Though parents are often in a hurry when leaving their child in the morning or picking him up at night, these times are appropriate for developing a trusting relationship. Congenial sentences informing the parent what her child will be doing are reassuring to both the parent and the child.

"Mrs. Nelson, Sam will be finger painting with shaving cream today. Sounds like fun, doesn't it?"

These comments are sufficient to start the child's and parent's day positively. That afternoon, the teacher follows up with comments describing the child's activity.

GREGORY WILMES, AGE 7.

"Sam had fun finger painting. He put cinnamon in the shaving cream and demonstrated self-control by keeping the shaving cream on the table. He's quite a boy!"

Teachers avoid telling parents about disruptive incidents. If it is necessary to discuss a problem, a conference is scheduled. At the end of the school day, the teacher's goal is to help the parent and child leave the center in an optimistic frame of mind. Both parent and child need time to love and appreciate each other. Love and appreciation are fostered by positive daily contacts.

Telephone Call

After an environment of trust has been established among the child, parent, and teacher, the telephone call is an appropriate resource for parent/teacher communication. Some teachers set aside a specific time for telephoning parents. This plan allows them to communicate on a regular basis and provides an opportunity to discuss the child's positive signs of growth, as well as any signals that indicate a lack of growth.

When parents receive a call on a regular basis, they are not alarmed when the teacher phones. The first several minutes of the telephone conversation are not spent wondering why the teacher is calling. The conversation is focused on the child. The teacher also

146

MELINDA NEUHAUSER, AGE 9.

informs parents of the best times for them to call her. This way parents do not call when the teacher is in class with the children.

Parent/teacher communication creates an environment of mutual support. When a problem occurs, they build on this trusting relationship. The following case presents a good example: Unis cries as her mother leaves the center. Unis has been coming to school for a year, but she was home all of last week. Leaving her mother to return to school is difficult for Unis. Her mother stays for a while, but when she does leave, Unis cries. Paul Star, the teacher, feels that Unis will be all right. He tells Unis's mom that she can leave and that he will call her. He says, "If you do not hear from me in the morning, I will call during my telephone time and we'll discuss Unis's day."

The telephone call provides the teacher with a vehicle for supporting the child's, the parent's, and the teacher's growth. A sense of trust and inner control is generated when significant adults communicate regularly and support the growth of the child's self-concept and internal discipline.

Parent/Teacher Conference

The parent/teacher partnership sustains a secure environment for nurturing the child's self-discipline. It comes to fruition during the parent/teacher conference. The conference is a process. Both parties have an active role in the outcome. The conference provides both parents and teacher with a deeper understanding of the child's world. They discuss anticipated or actual growth hurdles, areas of increasing competence, and joyful "kid" experiences. The process allows differing viewpoints to be expressed and similar attitudes to be consolidated. The conference is the growth arena for the circle of support.

Usually the teacher has met the parent or parents prior to the formal conference. These meetings provide the teacher with an image of the child's family. She has a basis for planning the conference. Successful conferences do not just happen. Like productive teaching, they require preparation.

Preparing for the Conference

Many teachers enjoy talking with parents. However, it is not uncommon for teachers to feel nervous and stressful about parent/teacher conferences. The teacher who is more at ease with children than adults should realize that this is a normal feeling. The best way to cope with these anxious feelings is to prepare carefully for the conference. Time allotted to preparation is time well spent. It allows the teacher to enter the conference with a sense of confidence and professionalism. Conducting parent/teacher conferences in a well-planned and thoughtful manner helps the teacher to grow as a person and a professional.

It is important for the teacher to realize that parent/teacher conferences can also be stressful for parents. Understanding this, the teacher prepares a pleasant environment for the conference. Comfortable surroundings help the parents to feel welcome and at ease. Specific suggestions for preparing the environment include the following:

- Have a neat, colorful room with numerous examples of children's work displayed.
- Have artwork displayed where parents can enjoy it while waiting.
- Have a pot of coffee or other beverage available to drink before and during the conference.
- Have an adult-sized table with full-sized chairs. A small round table is preferable.

In addition to preparing the physical environment, the teacher sets the emotional climate. Whenever possible, teachers should send home a short questionnaire one week prior to the conference. The questionnaire contains four or five questions for parents to consider. When the content of these questions begins the conference, the parent is immediately involved. Parents who have considered these points prior to the conference are prepared with answers and can enter the discussion with confidence. By beginning the conversation with parental information, the teacher implies, "I value your input about this child."

Parent/teacher conferences are appropriate times to use the information gathered in anecdotal records or through observation. If a school conducts formal or informal skills evaluation, this information is also available. Other informative materials, such as artwork, projects, or favorite books, can be on hand to share with parents. All of this information is compiled and placed in a folder before the parents arrive.

Conducting the Conference

The teacher who has prepared in the above manner has set the tone for a meaningful parent/teacher conference. When the parents enter the room, the teacher walks toward them and greets them. If they have not had the opportunity to get a beverage, this is an appropriate time to suggest it. The teacher then invites the parents to be seated at the table. The teacher sits next to or at a right angle to parents, not across from them.

It is important to keep in mind that this is a parent/teacher conference, not a teacher-only conference. Parents know their child and have a lot of information to share.

If a questionnaire was sent home prior to the conference, the teacher begins by referring to the information on the questionnaire. She may say, "I see that your family enjoys camping. What does Michael like to do on a camping trip?" By demonstrating interest in what parents have to say, the teacher learns much about how this child is motivated and how he spends his out-of-school time. Knowing these things helps a teacher to understand why the child behaves as he does at school. The door is now open for parents to voice their concerns. They are usually more willing to ask questions if they have been listened to first.

If the teacher did not send home a questionnaire, she can begin by relating a positive incident about the child. This assures parents that the teacher really does care about their child. This also sets a positive direction for the conference. Many parents view a conference as a time when they will hear "bad" things about their child. A positive beginning dispels this assumption and puts parents at ease.

The teacher has now set the tone for the conference, and parents realize that this is a team effort meant to help their child. They are ready to listen. Now is the time to open the folder of collected materials. Parents want to hear "good" things about their child, but they are also realistic and can handle the child's limitations. It is, however, best to begin with something nonthreatening, such as the child's artwork. Anecdotal records and other information concerning the development of the child can be discussed next. The teacher will want to take time to explain how records are kept and what is done with the information. Confidentiality is stressed. Parents are interested to hear how this information helps make each day as beneficial as possible for their child. The teacher explains that this information is the basis for the daily lesson plan.

When presenting the information, the teacher needs to speak in words that parents understand. If an educational term, such as "anecdotal records," is used, it should be explained immediately rather than leaving parents to guess what the teacher means. Undefined "educational jargon" makes people feel uncomfortable. Parents want to understand, but they have different occupations and are not familiar with "educationese."

Before the conference, the teacher gathers all the information and considers how to present it in a tactful and honest manner. The best way to do this is to be factual and objective, describing the child's behavior at school. It is necessary to avoid using words that are judgmental. When behavior is described objectively, parents are able to draw their own conclusions and to work with the teacher to find solutions. When a teacher uses subjective, judgmental terms, parents may become defensive or angry. The following examples illustrate what is meant by objective descriptions of behavior.

Instead of saying, "Leon is stubborn," a teacher might say, "Generally, at clean-up time Leon continues to play. I speak to him about the need to put the toys away, but he continues with his project. I am trying to find a way to help him understand that I value his interest in his work but that he needs to be willing to stop at the required time in order to have a snack."

Instead of saying, "I am worried about Melinda because she is passive and withdrawn, and she doesn't have any friends," a teacher could say, "Let me describe a typical day for you. Melinda comes into school, hangs up her coat, and goes right to the art table. She works at a drawing or collage for about a half hour without talking, then goes to the small rocker and rocks for fifteen to twenty minutes."

These examples illustrate how a description of behavior allows parents to see for themselves the problems that are emerging. Often, they see similar behaviors at home and will welcome professional suggestions about how to work with the child. When the

home and school take a similar approach, solutions are more likely
to be found.

Most people tend to incorporate judgmental terms into their conversations. Changing this pattern takes time and self-discipline. A
teacher who decides to work at describing children's behavior as
objectively as possible needs to be patient with herself. As is done
in creative problem solving, it can be helpful to "act out" a conference ahead of time. Two teachers can "practice" for their more difficult conferences by role playing. One teacher takes the role of the
parent. It is beneficial to role play the conference in different ways.
The "parent" could respond by being withdrawn, then angry, and
then cooperative. This technique prepares a teacher to deal effectively with a variety of parental responses.

The conference is ended with the reassurance that the teacher
will be in contact with parents to keep them informed about their
child's progress. The teacher encourages parents to keep her informed about what is happening at home. And the teacher reassures the parent that she will do the same. The parents leave with
the knowledge that this is a team effort.

Conclusion

Children, parents, and teachers all learn and grow in an atmosphere of mutual support. When teachers provide parents with
written materials, visual communication, and personal interaction,
they articulate the environment of discipline and demonstrate trust.
The parent/teacher conference is the culminating aspect of this
nurturing relationship. When teachers and parents are able to establish and maintain an accurate and accepting relationship, to
communicate in nonjudgmental terms, and to work together to support the child's growth, they have successfully extended the environment of discipline and drawn one another into the circle of
support.

Practical Discipline

Early childhood educators work hard to establish the environment of discipline. They base their work on an understanding of human development. They carefully prepare the physical environment and plan a stimulating curriculum. Teachers model, support, and correct their own growth, as well as the children's. Teachers instruct children in the art of self-discipline by establishing trust, encouraging creative play, and teaching creative problem solving. They communicate with parents.

When these steps are taken, growth occurs and self-discipline emerges. However, the teacher with an accurate and accepting concept of herself and others does not expect perfection. She is not surprised when, in spite of careful preparation, the classroom becomes disrupted.

The appendix offers practical suggestions for preventing and correcting these difficult times. Six specific times of day are examined—independent exploration, clean-up, transitions, group time, beginnings, and endings.

Independent Exploration

Miss Jeanne's favorite time of the day is independent exploration. During this time, the children are able to work at activities of their own choosing. Miss Jeanne works with individual children and small groups. One day the children are involved in their play, each child enjoying a chosen activity. Miss Jeanne joins the children in the block center. She sits down and enters into the play. After about ten minutes, she looks up from the block play and sees that the classroom has dissolved into chaos. Most of the children who had been so involved just several minutes ago are now behaving inappropriately.

"Oh, no!" she thinks. "How could I have let this happen? What will I do to calm everyone down?" Regaining her composure, Miss Jeanne decides to take the children to the outdoor center. When

152

they return to the classroom, about a half hour later, they clean up the materials that had been left out.

In the above example, Miss Jeanne became so engrossed in her block play that she was not aware of the activity in the remainder of the classroom. She neglected to position herself with her back to the wall, so that she could periodically scan the room. She was not "with it."

This type of experience can be frustrating to any teacher. Preventive discipline eliminates most classroom problems. Yet, every teacher experiences times when the class becomes out of control. When this happens, a teacher has several alternatives.

A Signal

A signal that means "quiet down" is established with the children at the beginning of the school year. Whenever the noise level becomes too high, the teacher simply gives the signal, and the children know that they need to lower their voices. The value of a signal is that it eliminates the need for the teacher to raise her voice. Several possible signals are as follows: playing several notes on the piano, raising one hand and walking around the room, ringing a bell, slowly flashing the lights.

A Walk

Like Miss Jeanne, the teacher may decide to take the children outside to play. Alternatives are to take a walk around the school building, through the neighborhood, or to a local playground. A walk outside allows the children to "get their wiggles out."

A Drum

The teacher slowly walks around the room beating a drum. As she passes a child, he stops what he is doing and begins to beat his thighs like a drum. Soon all of the children are playing "drums" along with the teacher. When the teacher feels that the children are involved in this activity, she beats her drum softer and softer. The children follow. Soon all of the drums are quiet, and the children resume their activities.

Freeze

Using one of the children's favorite songs, the teacher begins a game of Freeze. When the music begins, the children stop what they are doing and dance to the music. When the music stops (the teacher lifts the needle off the record), the children "freeze." The music resumes and the children dance. The game ends with the children in a freeze position. The teacher quickly and quietly goes to each child and encourages him to return to his activity in a quiet manner.

A Song

The teacher walks around the room singing a new song the children are learning. She encourages everyone to sing along as they play. Soon all the children are singing. Gradually, the singing becomes quieter. When the song is just above a whisper, the teacher instructs the children to return to their play.

Follow the Leader

The teacher begins a game of follow-the-leader through the classroom. Each child simply stops what he is doing and falls into line as it comes past him. The teacher is very active. When she feels that the children have worked off their excess energy, she quiets the game down, relaxes the children, and asks them to resume their play.

ELSPETH STOWE, AGE 9.

The therapeutic aspects of creative art have been illustrated throughout *Creating Discipline in the Early Childhood Classroom*. Creative art calms. It channels excess energy. It invites intense involvement and promotes self-discipline.

The teacher who understands the role of the environment and the curriculum in promoting the growth of self-discipline makes open-ended art available in the art center. She does not view group art as contributing to the development of autonomy and self-discipline. The following example illustrates the type of discipline problems that occur during a group art situation.

Doug Bradley gives the signal for the children to clean up the classroom and come to the art table for the daily project, collage scrap faces. Some children come eagerly. Others come slowly. The children arrive at the art table at different times. Those who arrive quickly want to begin but must wait for Doug to give the directions to the whole group.

As the first children wait, they become disruptive, poking children next to them, kicking under the table, and becoming loud. Finally, all of the children are at the table. Doug quiets them down and gives instructions for completing the faces. He then passes out the necessary materials. Some children become immediately involved. Others start out in a half-hearted way. Still others seem completely uninterested. They listlessly paste some paper together and start to leave. Doug encourages them to stay but allows them to start another activity. The children continue at their own pace. Soon most have completed the project and have resumed independent exploration. Several children remain at the art table. They are not close to completion. Doug would like to remain near these children and help them finish. However, he feels that he needs to be supervising the others to prevent disruption.

Doug's situation is not uncommon when young children are asked to do structured group art. Doug solves his problem by eliminating structured art from his curriculum and replacing it with open-ended art activities available in the art center. Doug sets out the art materials before the children arrive. Because the media are open-ended, the children are able to work with the materials at their leisure. Allowing the children to choose when they will work on art increases the enjoyment and the learning. It eliminates the inappropriate behavior learned during group art. It promotes self-discipline.

Creative art opportunities are based on four types of media—drawing, collage, doughs, and paint. Each of these materials are introduced into the environment *gradually*. Teachers who define *discipline* according to its original meaning of instruction understand the relationship between the gradual introduction of materials and the children's ability to use them in a disciplined manner.

Drawing Materials

Opportunities for children to draw begin with crayons and white paper. Slowly, the teacher introduces colored paper and papers with a variety of textures. Next, the children are provided with pencils. Over a period of time, the teacher adds markers, colored pencils, scented markers, variegated crayons, chalk, and water crayons. She enjoys browsing in office and art supply stores for unusual drawing materials.

Collage

Collage materials are introduced slowly so that children learn to control them. First experiences with collage require paste, paper, and small pieces of colored paper. The teacher instructs her students in the process of putting a small dab of paste on the paper, rubbing it in, placing the collage item on top, and rubbing again. This method eliminates flaking and gives the children a sense of control over the medium.

When the children have mastered paste and paper, the teacher gradually adds wallpaper and fabric scraps, pictures cut from newspapers and magazines, textured papers, and ribbon.

Glue is introduced later. The children learn to squeeze a small amount from the bottle. The teacher frequently repeats, "It only takes a tiny dot!"

Once the children are comfortable with glue, the available collage materials are limited only by the teacher's imagination. Like the teacher who discovered banana tape at the grocery store, she is constantly looking for potential collage items. She adds sewing scraps such as yarn, buttons, and lace; wood scraps from the local lumberyard's waste can; safe metal scraps from the hardware store; packing materials such as corrugated cardboard; objects from nature such as pine cones, leaves, and seeds; and fine textures such as rice, sand, coffee grounds, or computer punch-outs.

The major guideline for collage items is *not to overwhelm*. The materials are stored in a divided collage box or individual containers like margarine tubs. Heavy items, like stones or wood scraps, need to be glued to a heavy base such as cardboard or styrofoam trays.

At holiday times a collage box is filled with holiday colors. For example, at Christmas a box is filled with red and green fabric, paper, and ribbon scraps.

Doughs

Most teachers of young children make dough available at all times. The therapeutic value of play dough is enormous. When children are angry, unhappy, frustrated, or upset, they are encouraged to squish, mold, and pound the dough until they have relaxed and regained self-control. When children are happy, they express themselves through this versatile medium.

A fresh batch of dough is made at least once a week. It is kept in plastic or a sealed container overnight. Commercial clay is an excellent alternative to play dough. The following recipes are useful.

Play Dough (a big batch)

4 cups flour
1 cup salt
4 tablespoons alum
2 tablespoons salad oil
3 cups boiling water
Food coloring (optional)
Mix the flour, salt, and alum together. Add the food coloring to the hot water. Pour the colored water into the dry mixture. Mix well with a wooden spoon. When it is cool enough put it out on a big table for the children to help knead with their hands.

No-Cook Dough (a small batch)

1 cup flour
⅓ cup salt
⅓ cup water
Mix flour with salt and water.

Sawdust Dough

2 cups flour
2 cups sawdust
½ cup salt
Water
Mix flour, sawdust, salt, and enough water to make a good consistency.

Cornstarch Clay (sculptures become hard overnight)

1 cup cornstarch
2 cups baking soda
1¼ cups water
Food coloring (optional)

Combine ingredients in a saucepan. Cook over medium heat, stirring constantly. When it is thickened like dough, turn out onto aluminum foil or a breadboard. When it has cooled, give each child a small ball. Let him roll and pat it flat. Cut out a shape. Put a hole in the top and let it dry overnight. When dry, paint with tempera.

Initially, the children work with the dough alone. Eventually, a variety of utensils are added, such as cookie cutters, popsicle sticks, rollers, and a small wooden mallet. Textures such as cornmeal, rice, or sand are added to the dough to give the children multisensory experiences.

The children eventually learn to make the dough themselves.

Paint

Paint invites self-expression and involvement. Learning to control the paint is a skill. Children who are able to control a variety of paints and use them to represent their feelings, experiences, or aesthetic awareness are engaged in the development of self-discipline.

Paints are also introduced gradually, beginning with thick tempera at the easel. There are many resource books filled with suggestions about how to use paint. The following ideas are intended as a beginning:

- Paint with watercolors on unusual surfaces such as paper towels or muslin.
- Finger paint on a variety of surfaces from smooth and shiny to bumpy cardboard or sandpaper.
- Dab paint using cotton balls or Q-tips.
- Feather paint on butcher paper.
- Easel paint on newspaper.

Colors of paint can be coordinated to the season, holiday, or teaching unit. For example in the fall, brown, orange, and yellow paints are used. During spring, the shades of green, ranging from light to dark, are made available.

Textures can be added to paint. Cornmeal, oatmeal, salt, sawdust, and sand are added to finger paint and tempera. Sugar gives the paint a glossy look.

Clean-up

Clean-up time in the early childhood environment is viewed as a major learning experience. Children learn to organize, classify, and conserve. They exercise memory, cooperation, and consideration of others. It is an excellent opportunity to grow in the exercise of self-discipline.

JENNIFER GILL, AGE 9.

The clean-up time is always preceded by a warning or alert. "In ten minutes we will clean up" or "Only a few minutes until clean-up time." The teacher is actively involved in the classroom clean-up. She moves from center to center saying, "It's time to put everything back where it belongs. I'll check back in a few minutes so that you can show me how neat it looks."

The teacher actively supports the child who needs help. "Cleaning up is hard work. It goes better when you can do it with a friend. Come on, I'll help you." Usually, the child who absolutely refuses to clean up will agree to scrub tables or an easel with warm, soapy water.

Ultimately, the children learn to understand that cleaning up is their responsibility. The teacher supports their ability to do so through her involvement and her honesty. She tells them, "Sometimes I don't like to clean up, either. Many people don't. But if you don't clean up your own mess, I will have to do it. How do you think I would like that? That's right. I probably wouldn't be a very nice teacher if I had to clean up all of your messes every day!"

Transitions

Transition times are periods in the teaching day when it is necessary for the group of children to move from one activity to another, as from independent exploration to a group time. It is important to establish routines for these transition times. Basic routines are varied in order to keep children interested and involved.

General Transitions

Remembering that 20 to 35 percent of the school day is taken up with transitions, the teacher views these times as opportunities to impart learning. She develops a repertory of games and activities to draw upon during these transitional periods. Her reservoir includes the following:

Creative thinking games. As children wait for what comes next, the teacher poses a problem for them to solve. The problem may be serious or silly. It should not have a "right answer." The idea is to encourage divergent thinking. Any answer is acceptable. The teacher encourages the children to "brainstorm." Some suggested problems are the following:

- Mr. MacGregor needed to water his garden, but he couldn't find his hose. What could he do? What else? What else? What else?
- Margaret and Bobby both want to paint at the easel. How can they solve this problem?
- What would happen if everyone had purple teeth?

Finger plays. As the group gathers to move to another place, such as outside, down the hall to the gym or bathroom, or on a field trip, the teacher teaches some new finger plays. Active ones are best. Active finger plays help use up the unlimited energies of the young child and help him to remain in control.

Johnny's Hammer

Johnny pounds with one hammer,	(Pounding motion with one fist.)
One hammer, one hammer.	
Johnny pounds with one hammer,	
All day long.	
Johnny pounds with two hammers,	(Pounding motion with two fists.)
Two hammers, two hammers,	
Johnny pounds with two hammers,	
All day long.	
Johnny pounds with three hammers,	(Pounding motion with both fists and one foot.)
Three hammers, three hammers.	

Johnny pounds with three hammers
All day long.
Johnny pounds with four   (Pounding motion with both
  hammers,   fists and both feet.)
Four hammers, four hammers.
Johnny pounds with four hammers,
All day long.

Bend and Stretch
Bend and stretch, reach for   (Suit actions to words.)
  the stars.
There goes Jupiter, here comes Mars.

Bend and stretch, reach for the sky.
Stand on tip-e-toe, oh! so high!

Singing. Transition times lend themselves to the singing of favorite songs. The children can choose what they would like to sing as they wait.

Creative movement. Moving from one spot to another can be disruptive. Young children have great difficulty staying in lines. These lines can be converted into a creative and active, but not disruptive, time of day, as the teacher instructs them to move in more interesting ways. A long line can be a train, with the children providing the sound effects. In the spring, children move down the hall like baby birds just learning to fly, ants crawling to their colony, or budding trees. Children can move down the hall like a marching band, a long snake, or a constellation of glittering stars.

"Fly away". To move children a few at a time, rather than in a large group, teachers use the nursery rhyme, "Two Little Blackbirds."
Two little blackbirds, sitting on a tree,
One named _____ (insert child's name),
The other named _____.
Fly away, _____.
Fly away, _____.
Go put your coat on to play outside.
(or, Fly to your cot to take a nap.)
The teacher repeats the verse until every child has flown away.

Gathering for Group Time
Usually a group time follows a period of independent exploration. As children put their equipment away and clean the room,

they come to the rug or "together" area one at a time or in small groups. It is crucial that activities be provided for the early arrivals at the together area. If these children are left to their own devices, they often become excited or disruptive by the time all the children have assembled.

If there is only one teacher in the room, she has several responsibilities. She supervises the clean-up and provides for the early arrivals by preparing the environment. As the independent exploration time ends, the teacher arranges an appropriate number of individual rugs in the together area. On each rug she places a picture book or puzzle. As the children complete their clean-up, the teacher says, "You may pick a rug to sit on and look at a book (or work a puzzle) as you wait for the others. Once you have picked a rug, that is your space. Remember to stay in your own space."

When there are two teachers, one teacher supervises the clean-up while the other teacher goes directly to the together area with the first child. The teacher in the together area engages the first few children in easy conversation, asking such questions as, "I noticed you and Paul in the kitchen. What were you cooking?" "You used bright colors in your painting, Anita. Which colors did you pick?" "Tell me about the block tower you built." As five or six children are gathered, the teacher begins a group activity. The other children join in as they are ready. Whole-body finger plays are active yet calming and make an ideal transition from independent exploration time to a more controlled group situation. The following finger plays are suggested for this period in the day:

Rag Doll

I'm a floppy, floppy rag doll
Dropping in my chair.
My head just rolls
From side to side.
My arms fall through the air.
Flop your arms.
Flop your feet.
Let your hands go free.
Be the raggiest rag doll
You ever did see.

I Am a Top

I am a top all wound up tight;
I whirl and whirl with all my might;

And now the whirls are out of me
So I will rest as still as can be.

Touch

I'll touch my hair, my lips, my eyes.
I'll sit up straight and then I'll rise.
I'll touch my ears, my nose, my chin.
Then quietly sit down again.

Measuring

I measure from top of my head to my toes.
I measure my arms—starting here by my nose.
I measure my legs, and I measure me all.
I measure to see if I am growing tall.

Me

My hands upon my head I place
On my shoulders, on my face,
On my knees, and at my side,
Then behind me they will hide.
Then I raise them up so high
'Til they almost reach the sky.
Swiftly count—1, 2, 3,
And see how quiet they can be.

Wiggle

Wiggle, wiggle fingers
Right up to the sky.
Wiggle, wiggle fingers,
Wave them all good-by.
Wiggle, wiggle fingers
Right into a ball.
Now set it quietly in your lap
And do not let it fall.

Yoga. Yoga postures are challenging and relaxing, and they lend themselves to the transition period. The postures children most enjoy trying are the simple ones patterned after animals. The teacher simply says, "Now we are going to become dogs and cats." She presents yoga postures to young children by saying:

- Dog—"When a dog or cat gets up from a nap, he always stretches. The animals are smart to do this. It is good for their bodies. To do a dog stretch, get down on your hands and knees. Straighten your legs and push back on your arms. Lift your seat into the air and stretch as hard as you can. Hold for a minute or two and come back down to your knees."
- Cat/Cow—"This is how a cow stands. Stay on your hands and knees and sway your back down, looking up toward the ceiling with your eyes and head. Hold. This is how a cat stretches its back after a nap. Round your back upwards and lower your head. Now we are going to change from cow to cat whenever I give the command . . . cow . . . pause . . . cat . . . pause . . . cow."
- Frog—"Squat down so that you are sitting on your toes. Work to achieve balance. Place your hands on top of your heads. Frogs in a pond begin to croak all together and stop together. I will be the director of the frog orchestra. When I raise my hands, all of the frogs will croak. When I lower my hands, like this, all of the frogs will be quiet." After several "symphonies," the teacher may want to let the frogs hop a bit in their own spaces.
- Folded Leaf—"You are going to become a tiny folded leaf on the grass. Sit on your knees and fold your head down to the floor. Place your hands next to your head. Relax.

Attention getters. Once the whole class is assembled, a quick, attention-getting activity tends to unify the group. The teacher barks out the following instructions like a Marine Drill Instructor!

"Touch your nose; touch your knee. Reach for the ceiling . . . higher . . . higher . . . jump . . . jump . . . jump. Put your elbow on your ankle. Put your head on your knee."
She varies the commands each time.

A familiar story. A familiar short story, such as "The Three Bears," involves the children as they wait. Those who arrive late are familiar with the story and will understand what is going on. Or going on a bear hunt is always an exciting adventure, and children love the repetition.

Let's Go on a Bear Hunt
The assistant and children repeat each line after the leader.

Let's go on a bear hunt.	(Tap hands on thighs like
All right.	walking.)
Let's go.	
Oh, lookie,	

I see a wheat field!
Can't go around it,
Can't go under it.
Let's go through it.
All right.
Let's go.
Swish, swish, swish.   (Rub hands together, like
                                        swishing through the wheat.)

Oh, lookie,
I see a tree!
Can't go over it,
Can't go under it.
Let's go up it.   (Pretend to climb a tree. When
All right.   top is reached, place hand
Let's go.   on forehead and look around.
                                        Climb down.)

Oh, lookie,
I see a swamp!
Can't go around it,
Can't go under it.
Let's swim through it.   (Pretend to swim.)
All right.
Let's go.

Oh, lookie,
I see a bridge!
Can't go around it,
Can't go under it.
Let's cross over it.
All right.   (Make clicking sound with
Let's go.   tongue and stamp feet.)

Oh, lookie,
I see a cave!
Can't go around it,
Can't go under it.
Let's go in it.
All right.   (Cup hands and make hollow
Let's go.   sound when clapping together.)

Golly—it's dark in here.   (Say this with suspense in voice.)
Better use my flashlight.
Doesn't work.
I think . . . I see something.
It's big!

It's furry!
It's got a big nose!
I think . . . it's a bear!
IT IS A BEAR!
LET'S GO!
Repeat everything backwards and fast. Wipe brow. Make a big
sigh of relief, "WHEW! WE MADE IT!"

Together Time
Together time is often thought of as a quiet time, when learning
occurs through inactive language games. However, too much sitting
makes young children restless. They need to move around. To
avoid this restlessness, the teacher plans to play active games during the together time. By careful and varied planning, the group enjoys both quiet and active experiences. Below are some active
games to be incorporated into the group together time.

Parachute Play
Parachute play is not only enjoyable and active, but it also provides an opportunity for young children to exercise self-control and
cooperation. Parachute play requires a lightweight parachute or a
double-sized bed sheet. When presenting a parachute or sheet to
the children, spend time introducing them to the various handholds, rhythms, body positions, and movements.
There are two basic handholds for the young child. One handhold grabs the parachute with fists showing (on top of the parachute), and the other handhold grabs the parachute with fists hiding
(under the parachute).
Rhythms are the most difficult skill to learn, because waving the
parachute is exciting. The teacher uses key words to help the children control the parachute appropriately. The three rhythms are
"slow," "medium," and "fast." In the beginning the teacher and
children practice rhythms without music. When the children are
able to control the parachute, they are ready to wave it to music.
In addition to holding the parachute and waving it to different
rhythms, the children can assume different body positions as they
work the parachute. The easiest position is simply sitting on the
floor. Once they have mastered the three basic rhythms in a sitting
position, they are ready to stand, kneel, balance on one foot, and so
on.
The children are now ready to add movements to their parachute
fun. In the beginning they walk slowly in a circle as they wave the
parachute. Movements such as walking quickly, sliding, hopping,
and tiptoeing are added.

When the children are moving and controlling the parachute, they are ready to play games. Recordings with directions can be used with the parachute. For example, a record where the music is fast, slows down, and picks up again is interesting. A record that gives movement directions such as tiptoe, hop, and run may be used. There are also Parachute Play records with music and directions specifically designed for the parachute.

During the holidays the parachute is used as a vehicle for movement. For example, the parachute is Santa's sled and the children the reindeer. They all "tie into the sled." When ready, they take off and race through the sky, looking for the first home. They land, wait for Santa to deliver the gifts, and then take off again for the next house.

Bean-Bags

Bean-bags are another form of active game that is as versatile as the teacher's imagination. Unlike the parachute, the bean-bag does not take much preliminary work. The only preparation is learning to pass the bean-bag. The children practice passing the bean-bag several times. Once they have developed control, they are ready to play active games. The teacher directs children to:

• Put the bean-bag on the head.
• Balance it on a shoulder.
• Hold it in one hand and balance on one foot.

As with the parachute play, recordings with different tempos can be used. The children pass the bean-bag around the circle according to the tempo of the music. Children enjoy games on records that have been specifically designed for bean-bag play.

Indoor Mazes

Children enjoy the challenge of a maze. Using colored tape, the teacher maps out a path for the children to follow. In the beginning it is as easy as a straight line. As the children develop a sense of balance, the line may zigzag throughout the room. The teacher can also rearrange the equipment so that children are challenged to go under the chairs, over the table, around the shelf, and so on. Once the children are familiar with mazes, they can help set them up and take them down.

Texture Walk

The teacher gathers about ten rubber dish tubs. She also gathers ten different textures, such as sandpaper, sand, rice, macaroni, carpet, and water. She puts one texture in each tub and lines the tubs up. The children take off their shoes and socks and walk through each of the tubs. Some children may need help with balance. If a child does not want to walk through the maze, he can walk next to the tubs. As he walks, he pretends to be walking in the tubs. The teacher asks him how he thinks the textures feel. He may touch the textures with his hands.

Beginnings and Endings

The beginning and ending of the day pose unique difficulties for teachers of young children.

Beginning the Day

The teacher carefully plans the beginning of the day to set a calm and peaceful tone. When the environment promotes quiet, active, and involved learning, the children make choices, exercise self-discipline, and engage in meaningful interactions.

The teacher decides how to begin her day with the children. Two options from which she may choose are beginning the day with a group time or beginning with an extended independent exploration time.

Some teachers like to gather the children together at the start of the day to greet them, describe any special activities for the day, and provide them with an opportunity to share their news. The key to this type of beginning is to allow the children to enter into independent play when they arrive. The teacher makes it clear that they will need to stop what they are doing when everyone has arrived. Some teachers like to limit the choices at this time. When all children are at school, their teacher enthusiastically announces, "We are all here. We can sit together and start our day. I have some exciting ideas to share with you." Beginning this together time with a good-morning song is an effective way to bind the group.

Other teachers begin the day with independent exploration. They feel that it is best for the children to come into the classroom, to choose an appealing activity, and to be allowed time to become comfortable, develop a meaningful interaction, and extend their learnings into the creative realm. During this time the teacher moves about the classroom greeting each child, engaging in personal conversation, and helping children make choices and become involved.

Whichever option the teacher selects, she completes all preparation for the day before the children arrive. She is then free to become involved with the children—to model, support, and correct.

Ending the Day

All teachers want to end their day on a positive note. A short together time before the children leave allows teacher and children to

LEAH WILLIAMS, AGE 4.

look back on the accomplishments and joys of the day. They review events, share thoughts and feelings, bond the group, and say "good-bye for now." A song at the end of the day provides for security and continuity. The following verse can be sung to any tune:

Our nursery school is over,

And we are going home.

We'll all be back on Tuesday. (Name appropriate day of the week.)

Good-bye, good-bye, good-bye.

By taking this opportunity to gather everyone together at the end of the day, the teacher also supports the family/school relationship. When the child goes home and his parents ask, "What did you do in school today?" he has an answer ready. The ending together time helps the child to put the day into perspective. He retains an enthusiasm for what happened during the day. He transmits that enthusiasm to his parents. Parents see the value of their child's time at school.

Conclusion

The development of self-discipline is a complex and challenging aspect of human growth. Teachers of young children enjoy the challenge. They engage in careful planning or preventive discipline;

but when problems occur, they are not surprised and they draw on their understandings of human development and their ever-expanding repertory of discipline techniques. In discovering solutions, they support the inner growth of their children and themselves.